About the Author

Romeo Richards is the founder of the Business Education Centre, an institution that shows professional entrepreneurs such as doctors, lawyers, dentists, consultants, trainers, coaches, retailers and security firm owners how to attract customers and grow their businesses.

He has authored twelve books on how to increase retails sales and profit. He is also the author of the "How to effectively market and manage a professional firm" series for doctors, lawyers, dentists, consultants, trainers, coaches and security firms.

He is the creator of:

- How to Increase Retail Sales' home study course
- How to Attract & Retain Customers' home study course
- The Law Firm Business Growth Blueprint: Three Step Formula For Growing A Law Firm' home study course
- The Accounting Firm Business Growth Blueprint: Three Step Formula For Growing An Accounting Firm' home study course

- The Private Medical Practice Business Growth Blueprint: Three Step Formula For Growing A Private Medical Practice' home study course

- The Dental Practice Business Growth Blueprint: Three Step Formula For Growing A Dental Practice' home study course

- The Business Growth Blueprint: Three Step Formula For Growing Any Business' home study course

- The Restaurant Business Growth Blueprint: Three Step Formula For Growing A Restaurant Business' home study course

He has authored several White Papers and regularly writes articles on marketing, business development and retail profit improvement.

Romeo is a captivating speaker and a business growth and marketing consultant.

You can reach Romeo by emailing:
romeo@theprofitexperts.co.uk
or call +44 (0)20 8798 0579

"Dear Ann: I have a problem. I have two brothers. One brother is in advertising; the other was put to death in the electric chair for first-degree murder.

My mother died from insanity when I was three. My two sisters are prostitutes and my father sells crack to handicapped elementary school students.

Recently, I met a girl who was just released from a reformatory where she served time for killing her puppy with a ball-peen hammer, and I want to marry her.

My problem is; should I tell her about my brother who is in advertising?"

How do you feel about me now after reading my bio, do you still want to continue reading my book?

I am sure it brought the chill to your spine.

What type of person will want to marry a girl just released from the joint for cracking her puppy's skull with a hammer?

Just kidding it's not my story!!!

However, there is something very instructive about this exercise I will like you to be attentive to.

That thing is: selling is about emotion.

In most sales and marketing books, the authors try their best to give you tactics and strategies for closing sales and the use of marketing tools such as social media or direct mail.

What most of those marketing books lack that you will find in this workbook is the most important word in marketing…

That word is compassion.

You might be confused now, wondering to yourself, what does compassion have to do with marketing.

In order to effectively market to someone, no matter what you are selling, you need to communicate with that person.

You can NEVER communicate effectively with another human being if you do not understand him or her.

Think about the magical communication between a mother and a child.

A baby does not tell its mother that it is hungry or needs changing.

However, the mother knows instinctively, when a baby cries the reason it is crying.

And as the child grows up, he/she does not attend a seminar to differentiate between it mother and others, yet the child knows instinctively that its relationship with its mother is different from the rest of the world.

That is compassion.

Compassion is defined as the emotion that one feels in response to the suffering of others that motivates a desire to help.

At the end of this workbook, you will know how to develop compassion for your customers so that when they see your marketing message they immediately feel a connection with you.

There is a saying that you first need to win people's heart in order to get into their wallet.

At the end of this workbook, you will know the most effective strategies for getting into the hearts of your customers in order to get into their wallets.

The workbook is a component of the 'How to Attract & Retain Customers' home study course. The home study course contains seven DVDs, seven audio CDs and a workbook.

Purchase of the home study course comes with Skype and on site consultation and an invitation to exclusive private seminar taught by Romeo and other business growth experts.

How to Effectively Attract & Retain Customers

Including Strategies for the Effective Use of New Marketing Media

Romeo Richards

www.romeorichards.com
+44 (0)20 8798 0579
romeo@theprofitexperts.co.uk

Copyright © 2014 The Business Education Center
Print Edition

Dedication

I wrote about vision as your reason for doing anything. I do what I do first and foremost to be an example to my son.

Secondly, to have the ability to help my people shed the curse of poverty.

Alex this book is for you!

Africa this book is in your honour!

Acknowledgements

My sincere gratitude to Mr. White for editing the book and Paul of BB eBooks for formatting it.

How to Effectively Attract & Retain Customers

Including Strategies for the Effective Use of New Marketing Media

Romeo Richards

www.romeorichards.com
+44 (0)20 8798 0579
romeo@theprofitexperts.co.uk

Table of Contents

About the Author — iii
Dedication — ix
Acknowledgements — xi
Why you should read this workbook — xix
About the Author — iii
Dedication — ix
Acknowledgements — xi
Why you should read this workbook — xix
Introduction — 1

Module One: Overview — 4
Why do so many businesses fail? — 4
How to Attract Customers to Your Business — 18
Why Do People Buy and Why They Don't Buy — 25
Why Your Prospect Don't Buy Your Product or Service? — 30
Review — 34
Workshop — 36

Your Message: How to craft an effective marketing message — 39
Why Do You Exist? — 46
Creating an effective USP — 48
What Are People Buying? — 58
Why People Don't Buy? — 59

What Does Everyone Want?	60
How to Create Your USP	61
Story Selling	63
Steps For Creating Your Marketing Message	67
How to Craft Your Offer	69
How to Conduct Competitive Analysis	74
Summary	80
Make the Process Easy for Them to Buy	84
Workshop	86
Target Market	89
Education Base Marketing	96
Wow Prospects with Your Marketing	97
Systematic Referral Program	97
Convenience	100
Education or Training	100
Strategies for Segmenting Your List	102
Compiled Lists	102
Response Lists	105
List of High Leverage Prospects	111
Market Influencers	113
Workshop	114
Your Marketing Media	118
The Various Types of Marketing Media	121
Challenges Facing Your Marketing Message	125
What Next After It Is Opened?	132
What If They Do Not Respond	135

Website	138
Critical Questions about Your Website	142
Functionality and User Experience	143
Conversion the Critical Element of Website	144
Your Marketing Funnel	145
Conversion is Difficult	146
Lead Generation	153
Social Media	156
How to Measure Your Marketing Results	159
Your Need a Star	161
You Need Good Story	161
You Need Good Solution	163
Mathematics	163
The Two Types of Marketing	164
How to Measure Your Marketing	164
Workshop	167
Summary	170
Great Books by Romeo	180
Book Romeo	191

Why you should read this workbook

Two immigrants arrived in Germany on the same day.

With no knowledge of German, no technical skills and no work permit, they decided to find the only job they could easily do without the requirement for any of those: panhandling.

In the morning, they rose early, walked towards the city centre to start their job.

In the evening, they returned to their bedroom, which at the time was under the bridge. They just spread a cardboard on the bear floor and slept.

Luckily, for them, it was summer so it was not cold at night.

After two weeks, one of them had enough money to rent a room.

Six week later, he was able to rent an apartment and after another month, he bought a car.

Meanwhile, his friend could hardly scrape together enough money at the end of his working day to buy something to eat.

He was the one now feeding, clothing and lodging his friend.

His friend was very puzzled by this.

He could not understand what was going on.

He did not notice his more successful friend doing anything differently.

They panhandled in the same area; they woke up at the same time, started work together and left work at the same time and he did not observe his friend, engaging in any other activity.

After months of silence, one night on their way home, he could not bear the silence any longer so he decided to confront his more successful friend.

He said to him, 'mate, we both came into this country on the same day, we are both doing the same thing from the same place, and I don't see you doing anything extra, why is it that you are so successful and I am still struggling to make enough money to buy food. Are you a spy or are you doing something secretly, that I do not know about'?

His friend smiled and ask him, show me your sign, what is written on it?

His sign read: 'I recently arrived in Germany, I am homeless and starving, can you help me?'

And the more successful one said now see my sign.

His sign read: *'I only need ten euro to complete my transport fair to leave Germany'*.

Knowing something about Germans relationship with foreigners, some people were even giving him twenty euros to ensure he left their country pronto.

So he went on to explain to him that the Germans are not so thrilled with foreigners coming to their country.

So informing them that you just arrived in their country will not make them terribly pleased and be predisposed to helping.

The fact that he said he wanted to leave their country, they were happy to help him because there is nothing the average German person wants more than to see all foreigners leave their country.

(Let me make a disclaimer here, this is not a political statement against the German, I am only using this for illustrative purposes).

I have said before marketing is about compassion.

Everyone ones favourite radio station is what's in it for me?

Therefore, when you sit to create a marketing campaign, the question you need to be asking yourself is, what's in it for my customer.

How will my product or service make my prospects life better?

The majority of marketing campaigns fail because businesses fail to answer this simple but essential question.

The value preposition of many businesses contains only information of what their product or service will do for their customers and nothing relating to the actual benefit the customer will derive from using their product or service.

What's more, they do not even feature the benefit within the benefit, or the deeper meaning of their product or service to their customers.

Marketing is about communicating what's in it for your prospect.

However, effective marketing is communicating what your product or service will do for your customer.

What the immigrant communicated to the German was 'I want to leave your country.'

He understood very well that Germans will prefer every foreigner to leave their country.

So he tapped into that emotion knowing how good it will make them feel if he left their country.

What is the benefit behind the benefit of your products or services to your customers?

Does your marketing message communicate the deeper meaning of your product or service to your customers?

If your answer is no to these questions, then you have made the right decision to purchase this workbook.

This workbook contains a step-by-step process for crafting an effective marketing message that pierces through the heart of your prospects the moment they see it.

This is the only marketing book that shares with readers strategies for crafting an effective marketing message, identifying your target market and choosing the right marketing channel.

Introduction

To market your product or service effectively, picture yourself as having a stage.

On that stage, you have four things:

- You
- Your business
- Your product or service
- Your customer

However, you have a single spotlight and you can shine the spotlight on a single thing at a time.

What will you shine the spotlight on?

The majority of businesses will shine the spotlight either on their business or their product/service.

Some will even shine the spotlight on themselves.

However, businesses that succeed, marketing campaigns that are successful are those that shine the spotlight on their customers.

The question they ask is, how will my product or service make the life of my customer better.

In order for you to answer that question, you need to answer the question:

- Who am I selling to?
- What am I selling to them?
- How am I selling it to them?

Effective marketing is about:

- Your message: what are you selling?
- Your market: who are you selling to?
- Your media: how are you going to reach them?

This is what you are going to be learning in this workbook.

- How to craft an effective marketing message that speaks directly to the heart of your target audience
- How to identify your target audience
- How to select the right media through which to channel your marketing message.

In module one, you will learn:

- The reason many businesses fail
- How to attract customers to your business
- How to persuade your prospects to buy
- Why people buy
- What people really buy
- What people don't buy
- The five key objections to any sale
- How to craft an effective marketing message (Your USP & Offer)

Module two discusses the process of selecting your target market?

You will learn:

- The process of selecting your target market
- The benefit of selecting your target market
- Education based marketing
- How to systematise your referral process
- How to choose the right list to market to

In module three, we will discuss strategies for selecting the right marketing channel.

You will learn:

- The various types of marketing media
- Challenges facing your marketing message
- How to ensure your marketing message is opened
- How to ensure your message is read after it is opened
- What to do if your prospect do not respond to your message
- How to build a website that attract truckload of new leads
- How to use social media effectively
- How to measure the effectiveness of your marketing campaigns

Module One:

Overview

Why do you need to learn how to attract and retain customers?

There are two reasons why, you need to learn how to attract and retain customers.

The first reason is:

According to data from the various sources, 75% of businesses fail by their 10th anniversary.

Fifty percent fail in their first five years of existence, of the remaining 50%; 50% of those fail by the time they are ten years old.

I must repeat this point: a whopping 75% of all start –up businesses fail before their 10th anniversary.

So if you are reading this workbook and your business has not yet reached its 10th anniversary, chances are it might not remain solvent until it 10th anniversary.

Therefore, if you do not want your business to be included in the above statistic, you need to pay your undivided attention to what I am going to share with you in this workbook.

Why do so many businesses fail?

If you ask many of the previous owners of failed businesses the reason they failed, they will place the blame on:

- Difficult trading conditions
- The economy
- Government policies
- Their location – Etcetera, etcetera, etcetera

It will never occur to them that the reason they failed is *lack of customers*.

When you have enough customers, your business will not fail.

When you do not have enough customers, the likelihood of your business failing is pretty high.

When investors buy a business, what they really buy are the customers.

They don't buy the building or machinery, neither do they buy the talented staff; they buy the customers.

If a business does not have customers, no one will buy it.

So one thing you need to understand as you read this workbook is, the only real asset in your business is your customers.

If your business does not have customers, it does not matter the value of your building, machinery or professional expertise, you are going to fail.

You need customers to be able to deploy all of your other assets.

Case Study

Let me tell you a story to hammer home this point.

In a way, this particular story is the inspiration behind the program from which this workbook originates.

A very close friend of mind owned a Latino restaurant/club in Manchester city centre.

His restaurant was a unique and specialist restaurant that literally had no direct competitor in Manchester if not in the entire UK. People come from as far as London, Edinburg or Cardiff to his famous restaurant.

It was a restaurant with a famous brand name that is well known in Latin America.

The name had featured in Bond and many old cold war movies.

The venue was a restaurant, a club and a membership club.

As a restaurant, it was reputed for having one of the most delicious meals in the entire Manchester.

The club attracts lots of people because the atmosphere in the club was completely unique. No other club in the city is quite like it.

It was the only all Latin music club in Manchester. Also, the Latin American décor in the club gives it a Latin vibe. Then there was the Salsa dancing.

Watching the synchronisation of different Salsa dancers making their various Salsa moves is a sight to behold.

The membership arm of the club had about two hundred passionate Salsa enthusiasts who went there at least once a week.

I knew a lot of salsa dancers who went there to dance four days a week, 52 weeks a year.

Almost every Friday and Saturday, there was a Hen party made up of fifty to seventy women on average.

Sometimes there were more and there were times when there were fewer women but on average, every Saturday, there was a hen party of seventy women.

On the surface, this will appear to be a very profitable business, yet my friend struggled to make profit.

The question now is: why?

I had series of business growth and marketing consultation with him.

Every time we spoke, he kept asking me for a new marketing campaign.

He needed a new postal, new leaflet or new something.

I kept telling him that his problem was not customer attraction, but customer conversion and retention.

He already had all the customers he ever needed.

- Two hundred plus regular members
- Bookings of seventy women per week in the restaurant
- At least five hundred people per week in the club

To ask for anything more will be taunting the gods…

What he needed was not additional customers but a system for marketing to the customers he already had.

Furthermore, to put in place an effective system for converting and retaining the customers he already had and putting in place a referral system.

The goal of marketing is to:

- Generate leads
- Convert those leads
- Retain the customers

On the first of January of each year, my friend already had two hundred plus people signing up for club membership.

So every January he was sure of a windfall.

Every Friday and Saturday, he had an average of seventy women who went to the restaurant for hen party.

Some Saturdays there were about two hundred women. Some Fridays he had about the same number of bookings. And on Tuesdays and Wednesdays, he had an average of fifty bookings. Then there are those going clubbing. On a good day, there were about three hundred people in the club. And there were a lot of those good days, at least twice a month.

The most important asset he had at his disposal was the name of the business.

As I said, the business was so popular that people came from all around the UK to visit the venue. Every time someone visited Manchester from Latin America, that venue was on the list of their places to visit.

And I must add that Manchester has two of the most popular football clubs in the world, so visitor traffic to Manchester is high. Therefore, when it came to leads, my friend's restaurant was never short. His main problem was conversion and retention.

What he needed to do was retain the customers coming through his doors and find a way of upselling them.

For example, all the women who went there for the hen party never paid a return visit.

The food was great, the service was excellent yet they never returned.

That will puzzle a good entrepreneur.

You have seventy women visiting your place of business every week and not a single one pays return visit after their initial visit; it is something that should disturb any business owner.

It seems logical to me that if he wanted to grow his business that should be the natural starting point.

Why was he receiving seventy to hundred women every week and none of them return after the first visit?

When someone is getting married and she manages to draw fifty or hundred people to her hen party, it means she has a lot of friends.

What could he have done to ensure the hen and her friends return to the restaurant?

The second question he needed to answer was: what else could he have sold them when they called to make the bookings or when they arrived on the day?

When someone is getting married, there are many other services they need:

- Catering for the reception
- Decoration
- Entertainment – Etcetera, etcetera, etcetera

He could have provided Salsa lessons to the guests at the wedding.

He could have provided private Salsa lessons for the bride and groom before the wedding to enable them impress their guests on the wedding day.

The Salsa lesson could have been sold as an after wedding couples bonding exercise.

What about the groom, they do bachelors party right?

What prevented him from offering a bachelors party to the groom.

What about after honeymoon, birthdays or wedding anniversary dinners?

What about birthday offer for all of the guests?

If there is one thing we all have to deal with every year is this birthday of a thing even if we prefer it does not come.

What could he have offered the guest at the hen party to ensure they return?

What about selling them souvenirs, they will love a South America souvenir to show their kids and grandkids.

What about offering them discounted membership or maybe even free membership as part of their package to get them to return.

The two hundred plus club members all have birthdays, wedding, and other special occasions. Salsa dancers are passionate about their hubby.

What other Salsa stuff could he have sold to them along with their membership each year?

Salsa dancing requires special shoes, he could have purchased shoes at cost from suppliers and sold them for a killer profit margin. Some of them needed dancing cloth, special protective gear etc.

Least I forget they do eat. What discount could he have provided members along with their membership? What about membership referral program?

Do you see where I am going with this?

There were lots of possibilities for my friend to:
- Increase the frequency with which his customers bought
- Increase the value of purchase
- Increase his profit margin

Unfortunately, he did not seize many of those opportunities.

In the dying days of the restaurant, at that point, I was travelling a lot, whenever, I visited Manchester, and I went to see him.

When we spoke, he complained about the recession that was killing his business.

He had a recession proof business but he failed to see it.

The question is: why didn't he see all of those opportunities…even when I pointed them out to him…

Why didn't he view them as viable marketing options for his business?

And what were the mistakes my friend made?

His cardinal sin was not putting in place mechanise for retaining the customers he already had.

But his main mistake was thinking like the typical small business owner.

His understanding of marketing was getting customers through the door. What he did not understand was getting the customers through the doors was only the first step in the marketing process. The conversion and the retention of the customers is where the money is.

As we say in internet marketing: Frontend (initial) sales make you money, but it is backend (repeat) sales that make you wealthy.

His failure was he did not continue the marketing process after he attracted the customers.

I constantly see my friend in many of the small business owners I consult and coach.

The typical small business owner does not understand that marketing is his key function as the owner of the business.

If you do not have customers, you do not have a business.

There is a formula for effectively attracting and retaining customers.

This formula has been working for the most successful businesses for centuries.

No business that has applied this formula ever failed…never…

It is this formula I am going to be sharing with you in this workbook so you will not blow a golden opportunity like my friend did…

I will just make another comment before going into the formula:

The customers you are trying to attract are exposed to more than three thousand advertising messages per day. And it keeps increasing.

So to delude yourself in thinking your marketing message is the only one your prospect is going to receive in a day, is a dangerous trend of thought.

The average person is busy with their own stuff.

Your marketing stands between them and their objectives. You might think to yourself your product or service is a solution to them. They view your product or service as an obstacle to them achieving their goals.

So until you are able to convince them that you are indeed in their corner, you do not have a chance of getting through to them.

My goal in this workbook is to show you how to demonstrate to your prospects that you are indeed in their corner.

We are going to be focusing on three aspects of your business growth:

- Attracting customers
- Increasing the frequency with which those customers buy
- Increasing the value per transaction

Remember, frontend (initial) sales make you money, however, it is backend (repeat) sales that make you wealthy.

My goal for you in this workbook is to show you how to become wealthy.

In 'The Book of Survival' author Anthony Greenback wrote:

> *"To live through an impossible situation, you don't need to have the reflexes of a Grand Prix driver, the muscles of a Hercules, the mind of an Einstein. You simply need to know what to do."*

The aim of this workbook is to share with you the fundamental marketing skills you need to attract customers, clients or patients to your business.

It contains strategies, methods, tools, processes and templates for effective small business marketing.

Deep down in my heart I honestly feel the pain of my friend, he and his father worked so hard to build their business. To have had to finally walk away after almost twenty years of excruciating back breaking hard work, must be really, really painful.

It saddens me when I see businesses close shop in this age when we have so much information at our fingertips.

This does not have to happen to you, which is why I have created this workbook to prevent you from meeting a similar fate. It is my hope that you take advantage of it.

Reason Two: why you need to learn how to attract and retain customers

The second reason you need to learn how to attract and retain customers is business is hard.

But wait…if you have not been highlighting from the start, you really want highlight this point.

I am going to say something that might sound a bit controversial.

Most people are used to hearing, find what you are passionate about and create a business out of it.

As a result of this statement, many people rush into establishing businesses that they should have no business getting into in the first instance, which in the end leads to failure.

Business is about providing a product or service the marketplace wants…is willing and capable of paying for.

If you are passionate about something that the market needs, is willing and capable of paying for, then lucky you; if not, you are setting yourself up for failure.

Business is not about you, it is about your customers.

And let me break this news to you in case you have not heard it before, people are selfish.

Everyone's favourite radio station is: what's in it for me; not what's in it for you, but what's in it for me?

Therefore, when you make the decision to establish a business, you need to gain complete clarity about:

- Why you want to establish the business?
- Who you want to serve?
- What's in it for them?

We are going to dig deeper into these in the section about your marketing message, however, I needed to get this out before going any further into the workbook.

Case Study

As part of my marketing funnel (sales process), I offer free initial consultation.

When I get on the phone or Skype to speak to someone for the first time, the first question I ask them is:

If we are having this conversation twelve months from now, what would you like to have happened for you to say you have had a successful year?

Some people will tell me things like they want to have achieved half a million pound profit or turnover…The follow up question to this response is: What is your current turnover?

Well, I am just about to start…Is the usual response.

The following question is: How much access do you have to resources?

In most instances it is like ten pounds two penny plus their grandfather's old Volkswagen beetle.

'So you have no customers; No access to resources and it's not like you have created a revolutionary social media platform that will trump Facebook or created cure for cancer, yet you expect to make half a million in twelve months?'

But this is the mind-set and thought process of the many small business owners.

- Firstly, many have not clearly articulated their reason for existence
- They have no customers
- They have no resources for acquiring customers

Yet they set massive goals and they wonder why they fail…

If you are reading this workbook and you are in that frame of mind, I will urge you to rethink.

Except you have some type of revolutionary product or service, without the resources to market your business, you will be in the same position you are in this moment twelve months from now.

Do not listen to successful entrepreneurs telling you about passion.

They talk about passion because they lack the ability to deconstruct their process of success.

They are passionate about what they do because they are making money from it. Who will not be passionate about something they are making millions from?

They will not tell you the full story of how they got there.

If you want to succeed in your business, you need clarity about:

- What you want to achieve?
- How you are going to achieve it
- Why you want to achieve it

Business is serious.

You succeed and you are off to the races…

You fail and you may be facing the bankruptcy judge.

Your savings you might have worked for years might be gone…

Your house might go.

Your children's future might be on the line.

So business is not a game. Business is serious.

One mistake and you and your family could face serious consequences.

This is why it is very important that you give serious consideration to what you are going to be reading in this workbook.

You succeed, and you are lying on the beach. You fail and you and your family are on the unemployment line.

How to Attract Customers to Your Business

On my table here is my iPhone, I have it on a contract, and however, the market value of the phone is £500 to £600.

I also have a Samsung. The Samsung costs around £150. The two phones have almost identical functionalities.

In fact the Samsung has longer battery life and bigger storage capacity than the iPhone yet the iPhone costs almost three times the price of the Samsung.

Do you want to know the reason for that?

The answer to this question is the reason you are reading this workbook. It is only when you can answer this question will you be able to effectively market your product and service.

In order to answer the question, why is the iPhone three times the price of the Samsung, we need to answer two questions:

- Why do people buy?
- Why don't people buy?

Before answering those two questions, allow me to debunk one of the myths business professors have been drumming into the heads of their students since the beginning of time.

That myth is, the cost of a product is determined by the cost of bringing that product to the market. That is absolutely wrong.

The price of a product is never determined by the cost of bringing that product to the market but by who is buying and how it is sold to them.

To illustrate this point, let me tell you a story about an experience I had in Harrods department store.

Case Study

During the research for my retail books, I visited Harrods.

I have heard a lot about Harrods, but had not actually visited it.

When my sister visited me from the United States, Harrods was on her list of places to visit, however, by the time we arrived at the store, it was already closed.

You can imagine my anticipation and apprehension at visiting one of the most famous retail stores where royalties, Hollywood A-list stars and the "who is who" from around the world go shopping.

In my mind, everything in Harrods was made of gold.

I even bought a special outfit for the occasion to ensure I was in sync with the royalties and A-list stars.

I was hoping I could catch a glimpse of Roman Abramovich and some of his billionaire friends or some Saudi prince.

However, instead of some Russian oligarch or Middle Eastern Sheikh, what caught my attention was a bus.

I had bought the identical bus for my son from ASDA.

It was the same bus in the same packaging.

An odd question popped into my mind when I noticed the bus.

Why is it that the same bus, in the same packaging, probably made by the same people, in the same factory in China, being sold in Harrods for almost three times the price it was sold for in ASDA?

At first it was a mystery to me.

But as I walked around Harrods the answer came to me.

ASDA sells a toy bus.

Harrods sells classy toy bus even if it is made in the same factory in China.

There is a difference, that difference is this:

When someone buys the bus from Harrods, they are not paying for the crappy plastic that was probably bought in China for fifty cents; they are paying for the experience of buying in Harrods.

So the second thing I like you to highlight is this, people do not buy your product or service, they buy the experience and result they hope to derive from it.

And another thing you need to highlight is this: one person's definition or perception of value is completely different from another person's definition or perception of value.

Case Study

I do business growth and marketing coaching for small business owners.

Some of my clients want me to help them:
- Grow their business
- Increase their number of customers
- Increase their sales

When I go to see some of them or we have a Skype consultation on many occasions, all they speak to me about for the hour they are paying me, is their personal lives.

There were times at the start when I felt very uncomfortable spending their time talking about something completely unrelated to business.

But then those clients who I spoke to about personal issues were the ones who kept booking appointments with me each week.

I quickly came to the conclusion that they were not paying me for my expertise, they were paying me to listen to them.

This is marketing 101: people buy emotionally but justify their decisions logically.

Do you know which newspaper is the highest selling English newspaper?

Did I hear you say the Wall Street Journal or Times?

No mate you are wrong.

The bestselling English newspaper is British tabloid: The SUN.

I have on my desk this copy of the Sun for Saturday March 22nd 2014...

What is on the cover of the paper are images of naked women.

Interestingly there was a debate in the British House of Lords...The British upper house of parliament in which a female member accused her male colleagues of hypocrisy.

She said the Sun covered with images of naked women is permitted on the grounds of the House of Parliament while they have dress code that requires female members to dress conservatively.

I also have a copy of Cosmopolitan magazine on my desk.

Before your mind starts wondering about, I buy Cosmo to study their headlines.

Cosmo is the most widely circulated English language female magazine.

These are few of the best ever written Cosmo headlines:

> "His #1 sex wish: 71 guys crave this move...you want to drop this magazine and do it on the spot"
>
> "50 Sex Tricks: you will be the first girl naughty enough to try 43 on him"
>
> "Best.Sex.Ever.: out gutsy new tips are guaranteed to give him most bad ass orgasm imaginable and you too"
>
> "Weird Male behaviour decoded"

What you might be thinking in your mind right now is only bimbos read Cosmo....Ya?

You might be shocked to find out that it is women like German Chancellor Angela Merkel and Michelle Obama who subscribe to Cosmo.

Picture the German Chancellor walking pass the newsstand and sees a Cosmo title that reads:

> *"His #1 sex wish"*

Don't you think she will ask her miner to get it for her to try on Mr. Merkel that night?

This is not to like pick on the German Chancellor, it is only to make the point that we as humans, we are all first and foremost emotional beings.

When you are creating any form of marketing, you need to bear that in mind.

The Evidence

Dr Paul MacLean of Yale University developed the evolutionary triune brain theory in which he revealed that the human brain is in reality three brains in one:

- The reptilian complex: physical brain concerned with flight or fight
- The limbic system: emotion and feeling
- The neocortex: logical of thinking part of the brain

According to doctor MacLean each part of our brain operates separately from one another.

However, in most instances, it is the limbic system, the emotional part of the brain that is the most dominant.

So why did I bring up this theory?

Certainly not to demonstrate how smart I am...well sort of...Kidding!

I did to highlight the fact that when you create a marketing campaign or message, you are not only appealing to a single thought process, you are in actual fact appealing to the three different thought processes of the brain.

However, what most business owners or marketing agents do when they create marketing campaigns, they focus their marketing message entirely on the logical part of the brain...Especially when dealing with certain groups of prospects.

For example, someone selling to accountants or lawyers will create a marketing message to appeal only to the logical part of the brain because many people are wrongly convinced that professionals like accountants and lawyers are logical thinkers.

They are when doing their jobs.

However, when it comes to making buying decisions whether, it's for personal or business use, their purchase decisions are entirely emotional.

Every human being exercises the three parts of their brain:

- Physical
- Logical
- Emotional

When thinking and making a decision.

This is why when you create a marketing message; it needs to appeal to all three parts of the human brain in order for it to be effective.

There is a reason the Sun and Cosmo are so successful.

The editors and headline writers of those papers understand the triune brain theory better than other media outlets.

If there is a single word you must always remember in and about marketing this has to be the word: *compassion…*

Compassion is seeing things through the eyes of another human being.

Your marketing message can never be effective if it is not done from your prospect's or customer's perspective.

You constantly have to be thinking:

What's in it for my prospect or customer, not what's in it for me?

Why Do People Buy and Why They Don't Buy

Let's now go into why do people buy and why they may not buy your product or service.

According to the legendary marketer Jay Conrad Levinson people buy for 50 reasons. Learning some of these reasons will enable you create a marketing message that resonates with your target market:

The following are the reasons people buy:
1. To make more money – even though it can't buy happiness
2. To become more comfortable, even a bit more
3. To attract praise – because almost everybody loves it
4. To increase enjoyment – of life, of business, of virtually anything
5. To possess things of beauty – because they nourish the soul
6. To avoid criticism – which nobody wants
7. To make their work easier – a constant need for many people
8. To speed up their work – because people know that time is precious
9. To keep up with the Joneses – there are Joneses in everybody's life
10. To feel opulent – a rare, but valid reason to make a purchase
11. To look younger – due to the reverence placed upon youthfulness
12. To become more efficient – because efficiency saves time
13. To buy friendship – I didn't know it's for sale, but it often is
14. To avoid effort – because nobody loves to work too hard
15. To escape or avoid pain – which is an easy path to making a sale
16. To protect their possessions – because they worked hard to get them
17. To be in style – because few people enjoy being out of style
18. To avoid trouble – because trouble is never a joy

19. To access opportunities – because they open the doors to good things
20. To express love – one of the noblest reasons to make any purchase
21. To be entertained – because entertainment is usually fun
22. To be organized – because order makes life simpler
23. To feel safe – because security is a basic human need
24. To conserve energy – their own or their planet's sources of energy
25. To be accepted – because that means security as well as love
26. To save time—because they know time is more valuable than money
27. To become more fit and healthy—seems to me that's an easy sale
28. To attract the opposite sex – never undermine the power of love
29. To protect their family – tapping into another basic human need
30. To emulate others – because the world is teeming with role models
31. To protect their reputation – because they worked hard to build it
32. To feel superior – which is why status symbols are sought after
33. To be trendy – because they know their friends will notice
34. To be excited – because people need excitement in a humdrum life

35. To communicate better—because they want to be understood
36. To preserve the environment – giving rise to cause-related marketing
37. To satisfy an impulse – a basic reason behind a multitude of purchases
38. To save money – the most important reason for 14% of the population
39. To be cleaner – because unclean often goes with unhealthy and unloved
40. To be popular – because inclusion beats exclusion every time
41. To gratify curiosity—it killed the cat but motivates the sale
42. To satisfy their appetite – because hunger is not a good thing
43. To be individual – because all of us are, and some of us need assurance
44. To escape stress – need I explain?
45. To gain convenience – because simplicity makes life easier
46. To be informed – because it's no joy to be perceived as ignorant
47. To give to others – another way you can nourish your soul
48. To feel younger – because that equates with vitality and energy
49. To pursue a hobby – because all work and no play etc. etc. etc.
50. To leave a legacy – because that's a way to live forever

As you noticed from the list, about forty of the fifty reasons people buy relate to emotions.

The reason you need to be in possession of this type of information is, when you are creating marketing communication, you cannot direct it towards the logical brain only. If you cannot aim your marketing message for the three areas of the brain, lean towards the emotional brain.

Your customers or prospects do not buy your product or service. What they really buy are the following:

1. Solutions to their problems.
2. Freedom from pain.
3. Promises you make.
4. Wealth, safety, success, security, love and acceptance.
5. Your guarantee, reputation and good name.
6. Other people's opinions of your business.
7. Believable claims, not simply honest claims.
8. Brand names over strange names.
9. Easy access to information offered by your web site.
10. The consistency they've seen you exhibit.
11. The stature of the media in which you market.
12. The professionalism of your marketing materials.
13. Value, which is not the same as price.
14. Freedom from risk, granted by your warranty.
15. Convenience in purchasing.
16. Neatness and assume that's how you do business.
17. Honesty for one dishonest word means no sale.
18. Speedy delivery.

What your customer or prospects do not buy are the following:

1. Fancy adjectives.
2. Exaggerated claims.
3. Clever headlines.
4. Special effects.
5. Marketing that screams.
6. Marketing that even hints at amateurishness.

Why Your Prospect Don't Buy Your Product or Service?

Now let's go to the opposite: what are the reasons your prospects might not buy your products or services?

Why is it that when you make a phone call to sell something to someone or you try to sell something to someone face to face or through your website or advert they do not buy?

According to legendary copywriter Gary Bencivenca, there are five reasons people don't buy or what he called the five universal objections:

- No time
- No interest
- No perceived difference
- No belief
- No decision

When you send out your marketing leaflet, your social media post or create your website, these are the five reasons people will not respond to them.

Now instead of thinking of clever ways of tricking them into buying what you are selling, you need instead to be thinking of ways of addressing all five of those objections.

So how do you address those objections?

You do that by using the Bencivenga Persuasion Equation.

This is the Bencivenga persuasion equation:

> *Problem + Promise + Proof + Preposition = Persuasion*

It does not matter what product or service you are selling, you are solving a problem.

Therefore *problem is market*.

As long as there is a desire, want or need for your product or service, there is a problem that needs a solution.

So what you need to ask yourself is: what problem does your product or service solves?

This question is especially important for new or aspiring entrepreneurs.

Case Study

I always have certain conversation with business owners when they call to ask me to help them market their products or services.

The most interesting conversation I have is with professionals.

A lawyer could call me and say he wants to open a law firm and needs help with attracting clients.

When I ask what problems is he going to be solving in the market, nine out of ten of the times they cannot give me a concrete answer.

My conversation with them usually goes something like this:

> *'Dude I can see there are already fifty lawyers in your town, twenty immigration lawyers and you are an immigration lawyer, why should someone come to your firm instead of the other existing firms?'*
>
> *The answer is almost always: I am going to provide personal service bla bla bla…*
>
> *Do you really think the current immigration lawyers do not provide personal service?*
>
> *Or do you think someone is going to go to their firm and they are going to tell them we provide crappy service but you see across the road the new firm that just opened they provide great personal service.*
>
> *You need something other than personal service to sell mate.*
>
> *You need a reason to exist, that reason is what we need to identify before doing anything'.*

The Problem

So as you read to this, you want to ask yourself, what problem does your product or service solve?

This is because the first step in the persuasion process is understanding the problem your product or service is a solution to.

Problem in this context is not what you think, but what your customer or prospect perceive.

Sometimes as business people, we create a product or a service that we think everyone will love. When we present it to the market, we are disappointed that it is not embraced.

The reason for this is, we created the product or service from our vantage point without taking into account what the market wants.

I use the word 'want' because it's important that we understand that people do not buy what they need, but what they want.

Therefore, understanding what the market wants and creating a product or service to match your market wants is the first step in the persuasion equation.

The Promise

The next step in the persuasion equation is the promise.

What promise can you make to your prospect about solving their problem?

Taking into account the reasons people buy: fast, convenient, exclusive etc.

What is your equivalent of "Fresh hot pizza delivered in 30 minutes"?

The Proof

Thirdly, people are used to been given promises that are not kept, so what proof can you provide to back up your claims?

Your proof could be in the form of customer testimonial, list of customers, demonstration, sample etc.

The Offer/Value Preposition

Forth, what type of attractive offer can provide to entice them?

It could be price, guarantee or payment terms.

When you have those four in your marketing message or campaign, you will be able to persuade anyone to buy from you.

Those are the elements of effective persuasion.

Remember it is all about compassion for the customer...listening to the voice of the customer.

Review

Let's review:

What we have learnt so far is effective marketing is about three things:

- Lead generation
- Lead conversion
- Customer retention

We also learnt that we all have a three brains:

- The physical brain
- The emotional brain
- The logical brain

Therefore, when you prepare your marketing message, you need to be able to appeal to all three sides of the brain.

However, you must keep in mind that the emotional brain is the most dominant of the three.

Therefore, when push comes to shove, you need to appeal to the emotional brain.

You learnt Jay Levinson's fifty reasons people buy and Gary Bencivenga's five universal objections and his Bencivenga persuasion equation for persuading them to buy.

In the next section we are going to dive into how to create your marketing message or what most people know as your unique selling proposition (USP).

Workshop

1. What problem is your product or service solving in the marketplace?

_____

_____

_____

2. What is the price of your product or service based on?

_____

_____

_____

3. When creating your marketing communication, do you try to hit the three areas of the brain: physical, emotional and logical?

_____

_____

_____

_____

4. What promise do you make to your prospects?

_____

_____

5. What proof elements do you use to back up your promise?

_____

_____

_____

6. What is your offer or value preposition?

_____

_____

_____

7. When customers visit your place of business or when you clients purchase your service, what do you do to ensure repeat purchase?

_____

_____

_____

8. What provisions do you have in place to ensure repeat purchase after the initial purchase?

_____

_____

_____

9. What do you think your customer/clients consider value in relation to your product or service?

_____

_____

_____

10. Do you have compassion for your customers? Is your product or service created from their perspective or based upon your intuition?

_____

_____

_____

Your Message

How to craft an effective marketing message

One Saturday, I had an extraordinary life changing experience.

While getting ready to go out, I heard my neighbour banging on the door of my other neighbour.

From the urgency with which she was banging, I knew something was up.

So I ran down stairs to see what was amiss.

When they saw me, they both shouted come, come, come and help.

I ran up to pick up my phone, suspecting it might be an emergency and I might need my phone.

When I ran back into her apartment, I noticed her husband slumped lifeless in the sofa.

I felt his pulse…there was nothing.

I immediately dialled 999 and informed them; told them we needed an ambulance and explained the situation. They informed me that they had dispatched an ambulance.

I asked what we needed to do while awaiting the ambulance; he suggested that I start CPR before the ambulance arrived.

In the heat of the moment, my first aid training was out of the window.

So the guy on the emergency line patiently walked me through the procedure for opening his airway and administering CPR.

After a few rounds of CPR, the guy came back to life.

For me there was a feeling of ecstatic euphoria from recognising the fact that I had just saved someone's life.

If I had not run down as quickly as I did and taken control of the situation, it would have been game over for him.

His wife was busy crying. She did not know what to do; that might be natural, but the first guy she called had his hands in his pocket while he was on the phone.

When I arrived, I felt his pulse and immediately called the emergency services and went into administering CPR.

But the real hero of the story was the guy on the emergency line.

Despite the fact that I am portraying myself as this guy who showed up and took control of the situation, without the calmness of the guy on the emergency line, it might have been a different outcome.

Yes I had done first aid training but I completed forgot the procedure.

I could not think about how to start until he gave me instructions about how to go about it.

I alone without an emergency person on the phone, and it would have ended differently.

When the guy, came back to life, I was so elated that I even forgot to thank the emergency guy.

It was a few minutes afterwards that it came to mind that I never even thanked him.

Until this day, I don't know his name because I never asked.

The entire episode took a few minutes. It is taking longer for me to recount the story than the entire episode took…

That evening, on my way out, a thought formed in my mind that went something like this:

The guy in the emergency room who helped me had no idea what he had just done.

He had no idea he had just saved the life of another human being.

He will return home and get on with his life as if he had not done anything significant on that day.

In my eyes, in the eyes of my neighbour's wife, and the eyes of his children, this guy was a hero…he was the person who saved the life of someone, significant to them.

I thought to myself, I bet this is what the rest of the other emergency workers do. Even the paramedics, doctors and nurses, they save thousands of lives on a daily basis. Yet for them, it's just a job. They do not understand, what they do is not just a job; it is the highest form of humanity.

The only time you hear about the NHS in the news is when a doctor makes a mistake that resulted in the death of someone. Or when there is lack of proper care in the hospital that resulted in the death of a baby or elderly person.

As appalling as that may sound because every unnecessary death is unacceptable, those people save thousands of lives every day.

If the average NHS hospital counted the number of lives they save in a single day, it might be a thousand times the number of accidents or unnecessary deaths that occur in those hospitals.

Yet the only time the NHS is on the news is when there is an accident.

Granted, there are instances of evil doctors or nurses. But those are the exceptions, not the norm.

In a massive institution such as the NHS with thousands of staff, it is almost inevitable that there will be some rotten apples that will taint the name of the institution.

Even the BBC was unable to detect sexual predators amongst its staff.

Overall, the NHS is probably the best invention or policy any government anywhere in the world has ever invented.

So if the NHS is up there amongst the greatest of human inventions, why is it that the NHS keeps getting bad press from the media?

The answer is simple, senior NHS management lack the ability to tell their story. Like most businesses, they lack the ability to articulate their value preposition or marketing message.

All of the emergency services across the board are of equally important.

- The Police
- The Fire Service
- The Ambulance service

All are of equal importance.

If a gun was placed to my head and I was forced to rate them in order of importance, I will argue that the police is the least amongst them in terms of importance.

Many people might disagree with me. However, if they sat and properly analysed the role of each of these three, they will agree the man is right.

If you are sick and you are not treated in a timely manner, it could be game over for you.

If there is fire in your house and it is not extinguished, you will burn to death.

If a thief enters your house and the Police show up an hour later, what happens to you? You are shocked but not dead. You still have the chance to recover.

Think about this question: when was the last time you heard of someone in an emergency? A burning building for example and they called the fire service and they did not show up on time?

Or of an ambulance that is called for some who is dying; but does not show up.

You will be hard pressed to pin point times when the fire service or ambulance fail to show up when called in an emergency.

Everyone knows that you can never rely on the police showing up to rescue you in an emergency.

Many people have a story of times when they have called the police in an emergency and they never showed up.

This is not like I am disparaging the Police, it is a well-known fact.

Despite this well-known fact, the Police are more highly regarded than the other two emergency services.

Why is this, the case?

Answer…the police know how to tell their story better than the other two emergency services.

The Police force even has a PR department that spends tens of thousands each year to tell the story of the Police.

As you read, you might be wondering what my heroic act or the emergency services have to do with your marketing.

Well; everything

You see, effective marketing is about:

- Your message: what you are selling
- Your market: who you are selling to
- Your media: how you are going to reach them

In this section, we are going to deal with your message. In subsequent sections, we will address your market and your media.

Your Message

So what is your marketing message and why is it important to your marketing success?

Your marketing message is your competitive advantage.

What is your competitive advantage?

Your competitive advantage is an advantage that your business has, relative to your competitors.

The source of the advantage is something your business does that is distinctive and difficult to replicate.

Competitive advantage comes from providing unique value by drawing on special areas of talent and strength in your business.

Your competitive advantage is the core competencies you develop to enable you to serve your customers better than your competitors do.

Your core competencies are a unique set of capabilities, skills and expertise you develop in key areas.

Such as:
- Superior quality
- Innovation
- Customer service
- Team building
- Responsiveness
- Flexibility

They can also be the leveraging of proprietary technologies, information, relationships, and unique operating methods that provide the product or service that customers value and want to buy.

Creating an effective competitive advantage is very critical for any business, because there is no greater way to grow your business rapidly, than to occupy a strategic position in the marketplace.

Competition Between businesses is as much a race for competence mastery as it is for market position, market power and profits.

Developing a competitive advantage is like competing in the Miss World beauty competition. We the audience, have in our heads who we think is going to win.

The media have their own favourite, yet at the end of the contest, some girl from some obscure country stuns everyone by winning the crown. And, most people cannot comprehend reason for her victory. But she had a uniqueness about her that was invisible to the audience or the media.

Why Do You Exist?

In the previous section, I said that *problem is market.*

When there is no problem, you do not have a market.

Anywhere a problem exists; there is a market that needs filling.

As a business, you need to have a reason for your existence.

You exist because you do something that fills a gap in your marketplace or solve a pressing problem.

- Domino pizza solves the problem of getting food to hungry college students who wanted food fast.
- FedEx solves the problem of getting mail to customers overnight or same day.
- Google helps us to find almost any information instantly. We no longer need to go to the library to search for hours.
- Facebook solves the problem of connecting people.

At the beginning, I spoke about the amount of businesses that fail.

I said 75% of start-up businesses fail before their 10th anniversary.

Why do a whopping 75% of businesses fail?

Answer. The large majority of businesses have no reason to exist and many of those that do, lack the ability to articulate the reason for their existence.

When the majority of business owners think about marketing, the first thing that comes to their mind is the media – how to reach their audiences.

If the Yellow pages person visits, they will place their ad in the yellow pages.

If they receive a call from a newspaper, they will place their ad in the newspaper.

That is their marketing strategy.

I visit many business exhibitions. Displaying at those exhibitions is very expensive.

Yet all you find is people stood at the booths hoping that someone will approach them. They have no captivating message or offer. For them the mere fact that they have paid for an exhibition, they are doing some form of marketing.

But for any marketing campaign to be effective first and foremost, it has to focus on the message.

What is your marketing message?

Your marketing message is two things:
- Your unique selling preposition (USP)
- Your offer

Creating an effective USP

Many businesses avoid or struggle to create a USP because they find it difficult to differentiate themselves from their competitors. The majority of businesses are incapable of clearly articulating their points of differentiation.

Let me say clearly that **a USP is something you position in the minds of your customers or prospects.**

It does not necessarily have to be something tangible, it just has to be something they believe about your business. In order to create a good USP, you need to be able to answer two questions:

- Question number one: Why do you exist in your marketplace?
- Question number two: What problem are you solving in my marketplace?

Remember what I said previously, **problem is market**…when there is no problem there is no market.

In order to be able to answer the questions: why do you exist and what problem you are solving in your marketing place, you need to be able to answer the question:

What does my customer want and how can I give it to them?

Your USP is:

- What you do?
- How you do it?
- The result that your customer derives from it

This is how to go about crafting a USP:

Let's say there is a theatre stage and there is a single spotlight.

You have four things on the stage:

- You
- Your business
- Your product/service
- Your customer

But you can place the spotlight on just one of them at a time; on what will you shine the spotlight?

- You
- Your business
- Your product/service
- Your customer

The majority of businesses will shine the spotlight on themselves or their products or services.

Just think about this question, when was the last time you went to a website and saw text that read: are you facing so and so issue?

You can't because you hardly see that. Instead what you see are people telling you who they are or what their products or service does.

You visited their website to find a solution to your problem. You did not visit the website to learn about them and their products or services, yet all you see is about them…

What I am telling you here is this: *in order to create an effective marketing message, the spotlight has to be on your customer.*

Your entire focus has to be; what does my customer want?

There needs to be a *straight line* between your customers' wants and *your offer*.

How do you do that?

You do that by finding out what are your customer's wants, needs and desire.

How do you find out what your customer wants, need or desire?

You can do that by researching your market.

It's amazing how many business owners know nothing about their customers.

Let me give you a secret; if that's the only thing you get from this workbook, it will be worth your money and time reading it.

> *If you want to know how your customer feels, what thinks, wants, needs and desires, check out your most successful competitor.*

But here is a word of caution don't check out what they are doing now, check out what they did from the start to make them successful.

When most companies become successful, they drop the ball and stop doing the very things that made them successful.

From the start-up stages of many businesses, the founders do the right things to grow the business; however, as they grow bigger, they bring in professionals, Harvard business graduates who stray 360 degrees away from the things that made them successful.

So when spying on your most successful competitors dig into their archive and find the actions they took from their early days that are responsible for their success.

You will find a treasure trail of really good information about your customers' wants, needs and desires.

So the first step for finding out what your customers' want, need and desire is check out your competitors.

The second step is to check out trade magazines.

Your industry trade magazine and their industry trade magazine.

The third step is to check out social media and forums, see what they are posting.

Check out what your customers are posting about themselves, your competitors and the types of generic topics they are discussing.

Fourth, check out other purchases they have made. What they bought previously says a lot about them.

The Conrad Levinson's list of what do people really want:

- Happy
- Safe
- Successful
- Wealthy
- Liked
- Loved
- Have a sense of purpose
- Have fun
- Be pain free
- Eat tasty foods

Remember this list when considering crafting your marketing massage. People want what your product/service can do for them, not the product/service itself.

After you have gathered that intelligence, the next step in the process is to craft your marketing message.

> This is the equation for crafting your marketing message:
>
> What they are going to consume (the product or service)
>
> + Plus
>
> The time and effort they are going to put in
>
> + Plus

The three big benefit-oriented results that they're going to get.

Let's say they are going to attend training.

Following the above equation, the process will be as follows:

> How long will the training last
>
> + Plus
>
> How much time and effort do they need to put in during the training to understand the course work?
>
> + plus
>
> What will they be able to do as a result of the training?

The workbook you are reading is a part of a business growth and marketing training programme.

If you had the complete training, at the end of it, the core or primary benefit you will derive is; *you will be able to attract customers to your business.*

The secondary benefits are you will be able to:

- Market your business,
- Write and design good marketing materials
- Learn how to select your target market
- Learn to select the right media through which you can channel your marketing massage

But the title of the program and this workbook is "How to Attract and Retain Customers" because I know in the final analysis, your desire is not to learn marketing but to learn how to attract and retain customers.

Your message needs to be to be so *personal, clear, emotional, compelling, so benefit and result-oriented* that it literally stops your prospects in their tracks and gets them to take action.

There needs to be a direct connection between the *desire for your prospects, their emotional desire and the result or the outcome or the benefit that your* product/service offers.

That connection has to be perfect and the closer it is the better.

The more of a connection you hit, the more you draw your prospect in, the more you drive them to take action.

Furthermore, you need to ensure that your message appeals to the three brains:

- The logical brain
- The physical brain
- The emotional brain

But the emotional has to be the most dominant.

What you need in your marketing message is *emotional impact not so much intellectual impact.*

You need gut-level emotion that sounds *specific, instant, new, different, better, unusual or dramatic.*

How to Identify Your Core Competence to Use as Your USP

Different talent experts have come up with their own theories about using our individual strength to our advantage.

One theory goes that your weaknesses can hold you back from achieving your goals therefore if you have any weaknesses; you need to work to strengthen them.

Another theory advises people to focus on their strength and their weakness will become irrelevant. According to this theory, if you are very good at what you do, your weakness will not matter.

I am not about to get into the debate in this workbook.

All I want to say here is your strength can be a differentiating factor either as an individual if you are an entrepreneur or for a business as a whole.

Your core competence needs to be:

- Costly to imitate
- Rare
- Valuable
- Unique
- Durable
- Substitutable

To develop a core competence, you need to start with your vision for your business and the problem you want to solve.

Always remember, problem is market.

You also need to understand the strength and weaknesses of players already in the marketplace.

What uniqueness can you bring into the market to triumph even though they are already in the market?

In another section, we will address the question of competitive analysis, how to spy on your competitors.

Once you have determined your core competence, your vision for both your business and your customers, you need to determine your critical success factor.

Critical success factors (CSFs) are elements that ensure competitive performance.

In most industries, there are a handful of factors that determine success.

These factors are the critical success factors.

For example, your business could have a proprietary technology that it developed that will enable you to serve your target market better.

Many businesses are developing apps that are unique to their businesses.

If apps make life easier for the customer, then they can be used as a USP.

What I noticed is the majority of businesses are developing apps because it is easy to create and it makes them look good.

They do not understand that it's another thing in the string of things the customer needs to remember to deal with them.

Anything that adds to someone's to-do-list puts him or her off taking action because people already have a full plate.

So if your goal is to use technology as a USP, it has to be designed to enhance the life of your customers not add another task to their already packed list.

Case Study

I always have difficulties crafting a USP for professionals when I am consulting them because most of them are the same.

They attend law or medical school, graduate and just rot in their businesses.

When you ask them what differentiates them from the competition, they all tell you the same stupid things…They provide personalize service, they have friendly staff etc.

What they consider their core competence is either their competence or their transference mechanism.

When thinking of your USP, you need to think about it in terms of the value of your product/service to your customers.

What if, for example, an immigration lawyer specialises in a particular country, or a particular region of the world.

Imagine an immigration lawyer who specialises only in China or Russia. Can you imagine how much business that individual will receive?

Try telling an immigration lawyer in the UK to specialise in a single country; they will probably call the police for you.

Many professionals are lazy. Well most people are lazy but professionals are particularly lazy; they could be doing the same thing for years without any form of improvement.

This section is not meant as a professional bashing exercise. All I am saying if you are a professional, doctor, lawyer, dentist accountant etc. you can easily set yourself apart from your competitor simply by specialising in a specific aspect of your profession.

In one of Brian Tracy's programmes, he told the story of a dentist who attended training in Hong Kong where he learnt a single proprietary technique that was responsible for making him so wealthy; he was able to retire at age 50.

Specialisation or strength can set you apart from your competitors.

Strength is a talent completed with skills and knowledge. Skills and knowledge are learned relatively easily, but talent cannot.

Why is it important that you understand your own strength? It is very important because it enables you to understand others.

When someone buys your product/service, he or she is not buying what you are selling i.e. your legal or accounting services, the book or video.

What Are People Buying?

According to Conrad Levin, what they are buying from you are:

1. Solutions to their problems
2. Freedom from pain
3. Promises you make.
4. Wealth, safety, success, security, love and acceptance
5. Your guarantee, reputation and good name
6. Other people's opinions of your business
7. Believable claims, not simply honest claims
8. Brand names over strange names
9. Easy access to information offered by your web site
10. The consistency they have seen you exhibit.
11. The stature of the media in which you market
12. The professionalism of your marketing materials
13. Value, which is not the same as price
14. Freedom from risk, granted by your warranty
15. Convenience in purchasing
16. Neatness and assume that's how you do business
17. Honesty for one dishonest word means no sale.
18. Speedy delivery

What people don't buy are the following:

1. Fancy adjectives
2. Exaggerated claims.
3. Clever headlines
4. Special effects
5. Marketing that screams.
6. Marketing that even hints at amateurishness.

Why People Don't Buy?

Now let's consider the opposite: What are the reasons people don't buy?

Why is it that when you make a phone call to sell something to someone or you try to sell something to someone face to face or through your website or advert they do not buy?

According to legendary copywriter Gary Bencivenca, there are five reasons people don't buy or what he called the five universal objections:

- No time
- No interest
- No perceived difference
- No belief
- No decision

What Does Everyone Want?

What everyone wants to be:

- Happy
- Safe
- Successful
- Wealthy
- Liked
- Loved
- Pain free (and to)
- Have a sense of purpose
- Have fun
- Eat tasty foods

Most businesses often confuse features with benefits. It's important to differentiate between the two.

Features are the things inherent in your product/service. Benefits are what the buyer gets from your product/service.

When people buy legal services, they pay the lawyer to represent them, which is the feature. What they are really paying for is prison avoidance or freedom from legal entangle.

When clients pay for an accounting service, they are not paying for someone to do their books as most accountants think, they are paying for lower taxes and increased profitability.

How to Create Your USP

To create your USP, take a clean shit of paper and draw one horizontal line and three vertical lines.

At the top of the first vertical line, write the phrase: core competence.

At the top of the second vertical line, write the phrase: transference.

At the top of the third vertical line, write the phrase: customer value.

In the first box where you wrote core competence, now write the actual thing you do.

Example you are a lawyer, write lawyer and under that write the type of litigation in which you are involved and exactly what that entails.

In the second box where you wrote transference, write how you actually perform the task for the client.

Using the example of a lawyer here again, let's assume you are a criminal lawyer.

Here you will write, you represent clients in court or file appeals on their behalf.

In the third box, write the benefit the client actually derived from your work for them.

When you represent the client in court, it prevents them from going to prison, that's the surface benefit.

The benefit within the benefit is, it prevents them from obtaining a criminal record, which will damage their chances in life.

With a criminal record, they might not be able to get a decent job, which might ruin their chances in life.

So a lawyer's USP could be preventing people from criminal conviction that could taint their chances of a decent life.

This USP creation formula could work for any profession.

Let's use another example.

Let's say you are a consultant or coach.

You could draw the same three lines.

You first draw the horizontal line and the three vertical lines.

At the top of the first vertical line, place your core competence and under that list the things you coach or consult about.

As a marketing consultant, you help businesses to craft a USP or marketing message, identify their target market and select the right media through which to channel their marketing message.

In the second box, you write transference at the top. Under transference, write how you actually do the consulting. It could be one-to-one or group consulting, training, books or a training course.

And on the top of the third box write customer value. There write, client increase customer numbers, market share and profit.

Based upon the base formula, as a marketing consultant, what you do is help businesses *increase customer numbers, market share and profit.*

With this in mind, you need to understand that when you are creating your USP, your focus needs to be on the intrinsic benefits your customers will derive from using your product/service.

When I create my 30 second commercial, I do not say I help businesses with marketing; businesses do not want marketing, they need customers.

So I say, I help *businesses attract customers, increase their market share and profitability.* (You are welcome to copy it.)

Story Selling

Another angle to USP creation is the use of your personal story.

There is the saying in marketing that *fact tells but story sells.*

Since we were little, we have been conditioned to love stories.

Our parents read bedtime stories to us. At school, our very first lessons were all stories. The early conditioning has stuck with us in adulthood.

All religious books are written in the form of stories – think about the amount of people who have some type of faith, that's the power of good story telling.

Your personal story is the most effective way of USP creation.

We learnt in previous sections that people buy emotionally but justify their decisions logically. A well-crafted story can create affinity and bonding with your market faster than any other marketing tool, you might want to deploy.

The first time president Barack Obama, spoke at the Democratic national convention, he told the story of how his father left from Africa to US, how he met his mother and how he witnessed his mother die while she argued with insurance companies over treatment and entitlement.

His story is not only his story; it is the story of African-Americans, Latinos and foreign-born white Americans who formed the core of his constituents.

When you effectively tell stories that touch people's hearts, it is very easy to touch their wallets.

The Correct Structure of a Conversion Story

In Dr Robert Chadini's book 'Influence', he outlined 'like' as a key factor of influence.

People buy from people they like and trust. When you get people to believe you are like them, there is a high possibility they will want to do business with you.

However, in order to use your story effectively as your USP, it has to follow a specific structure.

The great mythologist Joseph Campbell studied mythologies in different parts of the world.

In his years of study, he discovered that there were common structures that all myths took, no matter the place and culture.

That structure formed the core of his book, 'The Hero's Journey'.

Your story has to start from your struggle…Then your acquisition of revelation or realisation…Then your struggle to acquire the necessary skill or information… Then how you made the breakthrough…Next, you systematise the process…Down to how you taught others and they achieved similar result.

In a nutshell, this is the structure:

Here is where I was…When I received an epiphany…I took action but it was difficult.

Despite the difficulties, I persevered until finally I made a breakthrough. When it worked for me, I showed it to others, they tried it and it produced similar results for them. I systematised the process. Now I want to help you with it.

When you create a conversion story using the above formula, your message is highly likely to resonate with your market.

While writing the manuscript for this workbook, when I took a break to eat and check my email, I saw this email from Seth Godin the bestselling author of multiple marketing books including 'Purple Cow'.

This is what the email said:

> *"It's a story about money*
>
> *Money isn't real. It's a method of exchange; a unit we exchange for something we actually need or value. It has worth because we agree it has worth, because we agree what it can be exchanged for.*
>
> *But there's something far more powerful going on here. We don't actually agree, because each person's valuation of money is based on the stories we tell ourselves about it. Our bank balance is merely a number, bits represented on a screen, but it's also a signal and symptom.*
>
> *We tell ourselves a story about how we got that money, what it says about us, what we're going to do with it and how other people judge us.*
>
> *We tell ourselves a story about how that might grow, and more vividly, how that money might disappear or shrink or be taken*

away. And those stories, those very powerful unstated stories, impact the narrative of just about everything else we do.

So yes, there's money. But before there's money, there's a story. It turns out that once you change the story, the money changes too."

I could not have made a better case for using your story as a USP.

So what are the actual steps for USP creation?

How to create your USP or marketing massage

The key things to remember about USP creation are:

Problem is market – as long as there is a problem to be solved, there is the need for a certain product/service.

Secondly, your focus has to be on how does your product/service make your customers' life better?

So what problems are you solving with your product/services?

The thing about problem you need to pay careful attention to is, many people do not even know they have a problem, neither will some people be willing to admit that they have a problem.

Therefore, what might seem an obvious problem to you; might not be perceived as problem to your target market.

Another thing that is worth paying attention to is your affinity to your marketplace can be a really a good differentiator.

For example, if I consult an immigration lawyer, if he is British, it is usually difficult to create a point of differentiation for him.

However, if he is also from an immigrant background, it's a home run, because all he has to say is I understand your problem because I am just like you.

His affinity with the marketplace is a very strong point of differentiation.

Women could use their gender as a differentiator. There are many businesses that are specifically aimed at women. Gay and lesbians could also use their sexuality as a differentiator.

Of course using your gender, sex or race has its disadvantages because it alienates other sectors of the market. But if your market is big enough say around the twenty-five thousand mark, it is worth the risk.

Steps For Creating Your Marketing Message

Step one: Determining your strategic position in the market.
Here is what I mean by this – On what special segment of the market should your business focus? Determining this involves infusing your business expertise with the problem you are trying to solve, and then designing your product/service to address those specific problems.

Example: Domino's Pizza's strategic position was busy students who wanted food fast.

Step two: Determining your core competence
You need to design your core competence in line with your defined market position.

Example: Google constantly tweaks its algorithm to provide fast information to searchers. If a website is slow by just a few seconds, Google will panelise the owner by not displaying the site in a search.

Step Three: Determining your supporting business model.

How will you deliver your promise strategic positioning?

What changes are you going to implement in your current business model to enable you deliver your promise?

Domino Pizza locates its pizzerias close to university campuses, hire lots of delivery staff and buys lots of motor bikes.

Step four: Determining your secondary competitive advantages

What other thing does your customer perceive as different from that of your competitors? It could be your price, pricing structure, guarantee, return policy, etc.

Step five: How to create your compelling marketing statement

Write your marketing statement in a few lines preferably two-five lines and then trim it further into a single tagline.

Example: "Domino's provides busy customers with fresh hot pizza and other food items, within 30 minutes or less. Our extra-large pizza and our value pricing make Domino's affordable to all customers".

Trimmed further to: "Delivered in 30 minutes or less or it's FREE".

When constructing your USP, you could start something like; do you know how…

Former GE CEO Jack Welch once said:

> *"If you don't have a competitive advantage, don't compete."*

Here is what Warrant Buffet the most successful investor who ever lived had to say about USP:

> *"The key to investing is not assessing how much an industry is going to affect society, or how much it will grow, but rather determining the competitive advantage of any given company and, above all, the durability of that advantage".*

How to Craft Your Offer

Your USP is only the first element in the marketing message creation.

To have an effective marketing message you need an offer that entices your prospect to want to do business with you.

In 'The Godfather' trilogy, there is this scene in which the Godfather asked a film director to cast one of his family members in a role but the director refused.

Every attempt at peaceful persuasion of the director had no effect.

Finally, the Godfather sent his boys to have a word with the film director in the form of his horse.

They severed the head of his horse and placed it in his bed while he was asleep.

That was enough to change the mind of the director.

Later when the Godfather was asked how he got the director to change his mind, he responded: 'I made him an offer he could not refuse'.

I am not about to show you how to send your boys to have a word with your prospects neither I am suggesting you kill their animal.

Those measures proved to be very effective in the security industry in the days before regulations.

One practice that was common in the security industry was to send someone to business premises in the day to seek a security contract.

For example if a security firm noticed a construction was about to start in their neighbourhood, they will send in their contract manager to negotiate the security contract with the site manager.

If the manager refuses, at night they will send their boys to steal some of the machinery or start a fire on the site.

That very night or first thing the next morning, the site manager will be on the phone to the security company.

That was the security version of the Godfather's offer he could not refuse.

As effective as the Godfather's offer is, I am not going to be teaching that in this book.

Instead, I am going to show you ways of devising offers that are beneficial for both you and your customers.

We are going to focus on ways of constructing a legitimate offer that will entice your prospects to want to do business with you.

What is an offer?

Your offer is what you use to entice your prospect to buy your product/service.

It is basically how you communicate your unique selling preposition to your prospects to entice them to buy from you as opposed to your competitor.

One of the difficulties of selling is making your prospect understand the value of your product/service to them.

Sometime you might have a unique product/service that you think is slam-dunk, and anyone who sees or hears about it will want it; only for you to bring it to the market and find yourself struggling to sell something you thought was the best thing since slice bread.

First of all, I used the words need and want interchangeable and deliberately because as entrepreneurs, many of us get into the habit of selling people things because we think they need it.

I have news for you; most of the times, *people don't buy what they need, they buy what they want.*

When I consult professionals, I am always amazed with their surprise at the fact that people do not want their service even though they might need it.

If everyone was buying what they really need, no one will splash out a million pounds to buy a Bugatti or Ferrari.

Does someone really need a Bugatti?

No, they don't but they want it.

Again, it comes down to understanding human psychology when constructing your offer.

What are the elements of a good offer?

According to Mary Ellen Tribby founder and CEO of Working MomsOnly.com a good offer must pass the following litmus test:

- It has to be specific: with your prospects understanding exactly what they get and how to get it
- It has to be exclusive – it has to be made to a select few not to everyone
- It has to be valuable – your prospects need to perceive your offer as valuable to them
- It has to be unique – your offer needs to be available only through your business
- It has to be useful – your offer can be exclusive, but unless it's unique, it's not useful.
- It has to be relevant – your prospects need to actually want what you're offering them
- It has to be plausible – some offers sound too good to be true, so that's sometimes going to make you look a little silly.
- It has to be easy to acquire – make sure you are offering to let them buy throughout the copy
- It has to be urgent – you need to have a deadline or early bird special
- It must have a guarantee: this, without a doubt, strengthens your offer

These days 'FREE' continues to be used as the new bait. Years ago, to deliver a 'free gift' to your prospects to get them to pay attention to your offer would have been ridiculously expensive.

With the internet, you can simple create an eBook, free report or video and use it as an incentive.

What many businesses are finding out is 'FREE' is becoming more expensive to deliver than even the paid products because every other business gives away something.

So 'FREE' is no longer a strong lead generation magnet.

If you do not change your strategies to take into account the new dynamics, you will be stuck.

Consequently, constructing an attractive offer requires serious thought.

Constructing an attractive offer that gets customers beating down your door will require you take into account the following:

- Your vision for your business
- The problem you are trying to solve
- Your target market wants and desires
- Your ability to deliver on your promise based upon your resources
- The result of your competitive analysis

Management great Peter Drukker once said,

> "The aim of marketing is to make selling superfluous...The aim of marketing is to know and understand the customer so well that the product or service fits him and sells itself"

A well-crafted offer is an offer that your target market immediately recognises as speaking directly to its wants and desires.

In order to achieve that level of understanding of your target market, you first need to know what is already in the marketplace.

How to Conduct Competitive Analysis

As Benjamin Gilad puts it:

> *"Behind every successful strategy there has been a tireless effort to collect intelligence".*

Strategy is concerned with what your business wants to do in the world.

Competitive intelligence focuses on what the world wants to do to your business.

I constantly speak to new entrepreneurs who will swear they have no competition.

If you have no competition for a particular business, it means either it is not a viable business or you have not conducted any competitive analyses because every business has direct or indirect competition.

Your competition might be other businesses in your niche who are trying to eat your lunch or other products and services competing for your prospect's money.

Therefore, it is very essential that you understand who and what you are up against in order to be able to create an effective offer.

Sun Tzu the great Chinese military strategist wrote "Art of War":

> *"–If you are ignorant of both your enemy and yourself, then you are a fool and certain to be defeated in every battle.*
>
> *–If you know yourself, but not your enemy, for every battle won, you will suffer a loss.*
>
> *–If you know your enemy and yourself, you will win every battle".*

You should at least know your competitors' offer to enable you craft an effective counter offer.

However, it's not enough just to know their offer; you need to know what their offers are based on.

Whatever product/service they are selling might be their frontend or lead generation offer.

Let me explain what I mean by frontend or lead generation offer using our business as an example.

Our business is engaged in coaching and consulting as our core business.

Sometimes it is difficult to enrol people directly into the coaching or consulting programmes. In order to get someone into our coaching programme; we stair-step the process.

We offer free videos and reports, and then we sell books, home study courses and workshops. It is during the workshop that we sell the coaching and consulting programs.

All through the other processes, we keep building trust and confidence…

Because we are using the book and home study course as a lead generation tool or frontend sale, we can afford to sell them at a loss.

If any of our competitors decide to base their offer and strategy upon our books and home study course prices, they will be seriously mistaken.

This is why it is very important that you study your competitors offer very well if you intent on using it as a template for constructing your own offer.

In order to analyse your competitors, you need to first identify them.

You can't shoot a target you cannot see.

After you have identified them, you study their strengths and weaknesses to find areas in which they are vulnerable: skill, asset, resources etc.

If you do not know the areas in which they are stronger or weaker than you, you will not be in position to compete against them.

You need to create a separate list for the successful and unsuccessful ones:

- This could be other businesses offering a similar product/service
- Businesses offering substitute products/services
- Businesses that could offer similar products/services in the future
- Businesses and products that might remove the need for your product/service

How to identify your competitors:

> Who else is bidding on your keywords on all search engines?
> - What sites come up as natural search results for your keywords?
> - Survey your customers to find out who they buy from.
> - Use your referral data to identify what sites your visitors are coming from.
> - Don't overlook word-of-mouth information from your customers and investors.
> - Don't overlook The Yellow Pages

There are lots of tools that can be used for a competitive analysis; they include:

- Way back machine
- Who's.sc
- Sophisticated search
- Your competitors' email
- Your competitors' customer
- Google AdWords and Bing PPC
- Your competitors' website copy
- Press releases
- Your competitor's products

You could purchase your competitors product/service just to familiarise yourself with their sales process.

Get on their mailing list to study their communication strategies, their promotions and announcements.

These are suggestions that might affront you. You might think to yourself, how I can buy my competitors product/service.

If your competitors get their hands on this training, they may be the ones buying your product/services and reverse engineering your process.

You should be all over your top ten competitors' websites, checking their copies, their links, each, and every page and the numbers of websites they have.

Conduct keyword searches on the major search engines and click on the first ten organic results and the first ten paid results.

Go to each of their websites landing pages, spot and note their keywords, sales funnel and offers.

After you have determined your competitors offer, you now assess your own logistics and delivery mechanisms, to see if you have the resources to match or exceed their offer.

I must repeat this point; *problem is market*. It has to be about the market not about you or your competitors.

It is quite possible your competitors might be doing the wrong things.

By that I mean their offers might not take into account the wants and desires of the market. So if you blindly follow them, you will end up like them.

Many large businesses are guilty of this…they are completely out of touch with their customers.

Your process should be to understand the problems, i.e. *wants and desires of your customers.*

Scrutinize your competitors to see how they address those needs.

Assess your own resources and with that information craft an offer that directly speaks to your prospects.

I will repeat this point; when constructing your offer, it needs to meet these ten criteria:

- It has to be specific – with your prospects understanding exactly what they get and how to get it
- It has to be exclusive – it has to be made for a select few not to everyone
- It has to be valuable – your prospects need to perceive your offer as valuable to them
- It has to be unique – your offer needs to be available only through your business
- It has to be useful – your offer can be exclusive, but unless it's unique, it's not useful.
- It has to be relevant – your prospects need to actually want what you're offering them
- It has to be plausible – some offers sound too good to be true, so that's sometimes going to make you look a little silly.
- It has to be easy to acquire – make sure your offering to let them buy throughout the copy
- It has to be urgent – you need to have a deadline or early bird special
- It must have a guarantee – this, without a doubt, strengthens your offer.

Summary

So what have we learnt?

We have learnt that an offer is everything your prospects get and what they need to do to get it.

Your offer must clearly demonstrate how it delivers on your promise to solve your prospects problem.

Examples of offers are:

- Payment upfront
- Payment later
- Membership
- Payment plan
- Early one-time discount
- Exclusive Offer – offer for certain folks only
- Limited Offer – scarcity-driven offer
- Limited-Time Offer – deadline-driven offer
- One-Time Offer – offer only seen once
- Qualified Offer – application required
- Combination Offer – combining more than two of the above

Compare all of your competitor offers so you can sweeten yours.

The core elements of your offer need to be:

- Features and benefits of your products/service
- Lopsided value proposition
- Premium/bonus(s)
- Risk-reversal
- Instant gratification component
- Reason why the offer
- Deadline
- Reason to respond now

Price presentation tips:

People don't like to be made to feel that they are about to spend money. Therefore, when presenting your price, you need to choose your language carefully.

Below are lists of ways you could comfortably present your price without it being perceived as asking them to spend money.

- Language (investment, etc.)
- When showing value amount use £97.00. When showing price amount use £97.
- If you are selling two different packages, sell highest option first
- If you have a "high" price, acknowledge and brag about it
- Build value, then present lower price point
- If you offer a discount, you must justify it with a reason why
- Test predictably irrational pricing…

When preparing your offer anticipate all objections. It will be good if we trusted each other and live happily ever after.

But in the real world, things are not that way. The one thing that people lack the most is trust, so you have to anticipate that when constructing your offer.

The following are objections to anticipate:

- Risk of financial loss
- Risk of loss of "face"
- Risk of loss of time
- Risk of inconvenience
- Risk of hassle or intimidation
- Risk of unsatisfactory results
- Risk of disappointment and frustration

To eliminate the objections, use the strongest and boldest guarantee possible.

Demonstrate to your prospects that you are taking all of the risk.

The following are a few risk reversal strategies:

- Conditional guarantee
- Unconditional guarantee
- Money-back plus guarantee
- Double-your-money-back guarantee
- Performance-based guarantee
- Time-based guarantee
- Lifetime guarantee
- Competitor challenge
- Unique/off-the-wall
- Keep premiums

The best risk-reversal terminologies:

- 100% money-back guarantee
- 100% satisfaction guarantee
- No questions asked
- No hassles guarantee
- Better than risk-free guarantee
- "We will buy it back!" guarantee
- "Try it before you decide"

Delay is the death of sales, so you need to motivate them to act quickly.

To prompt them into action, you could use the following strategies:

- Use real, believable urgency & scarcity
- Limited discount
- Limited supply
- Limited spots
- Pending price increase
- Beta/Market test
- Fast-action bonuses
- Deadline
- Remind them of their current situation (vividly)
- Warn of consequence of inaction

Make the Process Easy for Them to Buy

Tell them exactly what you like them to do. People say they don't like being patronised.

The reality is; the majority of people like being led. So don't fall for the stuff about people don't like being patronised. Patronise them, tell them exactly what action you like them to take in your offer:

Tell them grab your copy now…

Click the 'add to cart button'….

You will immediately be taken to….

Immediately after you enter your details and press the 'submit button', you will be given access to everything.

So, go ahead, click the 'add to cart button' below… See you on the other side.

By leading them through the process, you increase their desire to want your product/service.

Once you have identified your USP and constructed your offer, you can now create your marketing message with the combination of the two.

Remember: Your marketing message is the combination of your USP and your offer.

Workshop

1. Why do you exist as a business? What gap are you trying to fill in the marketplace?

_____

_____

_____

2. What do you consider your competitive advantage to be?

_____

_____

_____

3. What is your core competence?

_____

_____

_____

4. Do you gather intelligence on your competitors? Do you know how you stack up against your main competitors?

_____

_____

_____

5. What proof elements do you use to back up your promise?

_____

_____

_____

6. What is your marketing message, what are you really selling to your customer?

_____

_____

_____

7. Do you know your target market? What types of intelligence do you have on your target audience?

_____

_____

_____

8. What are your sales pipelines, how do you reach your prospects?

_____

_____

_____

9. As the founder of the business, do you use your personal story as a part of your USP?

_____

_____

_____

10. Write down the short and long form of your USP

_____

_____

_____

Target Market

We use to run free marketing orientation workshops for small businesses around London. The aim was to use the workshop as a lead generation magnet.

Lead generation magnet, meaning our sales pipeline.

We had to stop it because we noticed that the people we were attracting were not our ideal target market.

By this, I mean they were not buying; neither were they taking the action we wanted them to take.

At first I blamed myself, I felt my offer was not strong enough or I was not selling my services to them effectively.

The workshop was completely free to attend; I paid for the hall and all of the materials.

Whenever, we announced the workshop on Meet-up, social media or our website, we had lots of people registering for it.

Because of the number of registrations, we hired a big hall.

However, on the day of the workshop, only about half of the people showed up.

This went on for a few workshops; finally, we decided to change tact.

We requested a refundable fee upon registration. When we did that, not a single person registered. Did we do anything wrong? The workshop was still free.

All we asked was they committed themselves by making a payment that was to be refunded to them upon arrival.

The fact that not a single person took up my offer demonstrated one thing and one thing only, they were not my target audience.

We could have reversed course and changed the registration process to entice them into registering.

Even though we would have persuaded a few of them to attend, we were still going to be facing the previous situation, whereby they will register and never show up.

Furthermore, there was no guarantee that I would have persuaded them to buy even if I gave the greatest sales presentation ever.

Why?

Because I was trying to sell to the wrong market.

My consulting fees start from a thousand pounds. A thousand pounds might not seem a lot for a big business. However, when dealing with small to medium size businesses, a thousand pounds can add up.

Most of the time I receive calls from businesses that need help with their marketing; when I quote my fees to them, they receive sticker shock.

At the beginning I felt quoting the fees early in the conversation when I have not had the chance of establishing value was not a good sales strategy.

However, with time, I realised that if someone lacked the ability and the willingness to pay for a product or service, it does not matter at what point in the conversation payment is brought up; it is not going to make a difference.

Many professionals are always afraid of discussing payment in their initial conversations with prospects, they feel if they introduce price too early in the conversation without establishing value, it might scare away clients.

It is true that introducing price in a sales conversation early without establishing value can indeed kill the sales.

But there comes a point in the initial conversation when a professional needs to introduce price because if you don't, you might end up wasting hours doing preparatory work for the prospect, only to find out later that the prospects might have the willingness to acquire your service, but they do not have ability to pay for it.

For example, as a consultant or coach, once you have established your objectives, the metric for measurement and the value to the client. It will not be unusual at that point to ask the client their budget range or provide them an indication of the cost of your service.

If your cost range is way beyond what the prospect was expecting, you end the conversation at that stage rather than wasting time with a prospect to discover later they cannot afford your service.

This is a very essential component of successful marketing because anyone without the willingness and ability to pay for your service is the wrong market for you.

When you are trying to sell to the wrong market, it does not matter how enticing your offer is, you will not get them to buy.

I was smart enough to identify this problem and stopped my workshop. But many entrepreneurs and small business owners fail to recognise this fact.

In fact, the best direct response marketers will tell you that the right list represents 60% of your chances of succeeding with your marketing campaign.

You can hire the best copywriter in the world to write your marketing message, if it is sent to the wrong target audience, you are doomed.

A mediocre marketing message directed at the right market, you stands a chance of minimum success.

However, get the best marketing message to the wrong audience and you are doomed.

For any marketing campaign to succeed there has to be a *message to market match*.

We say in internet marketing, you need to find a hungry buying audience who are unreasonably passionate about what they are buying from you.

Whenever, you have to persuade people who do not see the value in what you are selling to buy from you, your campaign has already failed before it even starts.

When you have selected your market right, your marketing message will speak directly to them and repel other segments of the market to which you do not wish to appeal. This is a very counter intuitive marketing strategy because the majority of businesses are in the habit of trying to attract the broadest possible audience.

Why is it important you select your market well?

There are three reasons why it is very important you do effective target market selection:

Reason number one: Except if you are Nike, McDonalds or Coca Cola, you do not have enough resources to appeal to everyone.

Reason number two: in most instances, mass marketing is a complete waste of resources. For example, when you do mass mailing even to a targeted list, the best you can expect is a two to three percent response rate.

Now think about sending out masses mail to the great-unwashed masses, your response rate will be dismay.

Reason number three: getting prospect to become customers requires repetition, repetition and repetition.

In most instances, it can be very expensive.

According to marketing experts, only 1 out of 9 people will see your well-placed ad and it takes 3 advertising attempts to get your targeted prospects attention.

In addition 90% of all purchase decisions are made in the subconscious mind, which responds to repetition.

Which is why targeted marketing is essential because selling to the masses is an expensive preposition.

It is less expensive to send multiple marketing communications to a targeted audience than to try to communicate with everyone.

Yes everyone gets sick which means everyone needs medical attention but not everyone can afford to pay for private medical treatment.

One way or the other, everyone needs legal services but not everyone can afford to pay for legal services.

So it is just not possible for you to sell to everyone because everyone will not buy from you no matter how strong you appeal to them.

This leaves us with the only sensible option, which is a good market selection.

When you segment your market well, you are able to focus your resources.

Market segmentation is not just about targeted segmentation; by this I mean segmenting the market in order to know who to target, market segmentation also help you to focus your resources on the most valuable prospects.

What I mean is this: let's say you know a certain segment of your market has higher purchasing power than the rest, you can spend more of your resources targeting that segment because you know the profitability in getting to those customers.

However, you will not know which segment of your market is profitable if you do not know your market.

This is why it is very important that you know your target market very well and when you buy or rent a list, you ensure the list is well targeted.

The benefit of target marketing is as follows:

- You invest your marketing efforts and capital exclusively on marketing to your targeted, qualified prospects – those that are interested in what you have to sell (now or in the near future), and whenever possible are actively looking for what you sell.
- You can easily compel those targeted prospects to buy or at least try your product or service.
- You can afford to persist and educate them about the benefits you provide
- You can leverage off the new customers to generate other new customers through a referral program.
- You can expand those new customers buying patterns through up-selling, cross selling and conditioning them to purchase more often

How do you go about the process of selecting your target market?

The process of target market selection is as follows:

Market exclusively to identified targeted prospects

The basic foundation of target marketing is the realisation that it is far cheaper to market to your targeted prospects with multiple repetitions than trying to sell to the great-unwashed masses.

Let's say you allocate £20,000 for a marketing campaign.

If you spread the £20, 000 among 20,000 prospects who might need your product or service, you will be able to spend only £1.00 per prospect.

However, if you identified the 10% of your prospects who are most likely to use your product or service, you will be able to increase your budget per prospect by 900%.

However, the benefit of identifying your target prospects goes beyond just the simple question of your marketing investment.

If you can identify the prospects that use your products or service, you can produce far more focused advertising and promotional materials and offer that are more compelling and enticing to motivate them to buy.

Incentivise your target prospects to purchase or at least try your product or service

Some customers can be extremely difficult to reach. Or they may already have other suppliers therefore, are unwilling to change.

However, simply because a prospect is difficult to reach is not enough of a reason to give up on them especially if they are potentially a high profit customer.

So applying the concept of a free line will be the most effective approach in such cases.

Provide samples of your product or service or request a trial period to demonstrate the value of your product or service.

Education Base Marketing

The new form of marketing especially in the online marketing space where I came from is education based, marketing.

Years ago, giving away free products could cost you a fortune.

Today with the internet and social media, everything has become free.

Therefore, another way of connecting with your target market can be through the provision of educational materials to them.

It could be in the form of a video or eBook.

Providing your target market with free information will demonstrate your expertise and generate enormous goodwill amongst them.

Wow Prospects with Your Marketing

Have you ever attended an open day event where you are given VIP treatment?

Making your marketing process exceptional and mind blowing for the customer is another way of target market selection.

Put up an open day for only your target market and when they arrive, spear no expense to wow them with your product or service. The goal is to make the experience what it will feel like doing business with you.

Systematic Referral Program

You could provide a two for one offer to your new customers to entice them to refer someone else to you. Remember birds of the same feather flock together.

By providing your target market incentive to refer someone else, you will be leveraging your marketing resources.

Upsell and Cross-sell Your New Customers

Twenty percent of buyers will buy additional products or service if offered to them at the point of sale. So instead of waiting for a few weeks or months to introduce your other product or service to them, you can upsell or cross sell them at the point of sale.

What is the most effective form of target market segmentation?

There are lots of ways you can break down or segment your market.

Here are just four of the most common target market segments:

- By Demographics
- By Preference or Interest
- By Business Profile
- By Service or Product Level

Segment Category One:

Demographics:

There are six demographic categories:

- Income Level
- Age
- Gender
- Education/Technical Level
- Ethnic/Culture
- Location—Where Your Prospects Live or Businesses are Located

Segment Category Two:

Preferences or Interests:

You could segment by different interest and hobbies groups.

These include:

- Hobbies – art, trains, computer games, gardening, crafts and so on
- Sports – fishing, golf, football and so on
- Health – conventional medicine, alternative medicine, diet, exercise, chemicals and so on
- Education – training programs, books, computers, videos and so on
- Leisure Activities – hiking, theatre, reading, games, vacations and other activities
- Causes – environmental, social, political and so on

Segment Category Three:

Business specialisation:

You could categorise your market in terms of their:

- Market specialisation
- Products groups
- Service category
- Size
- Location

Segment Category 4

Service or Product:

You can also segment your market in terms of your service level or your product category.

You could segment your product or service into different categories to satisfy certain sectors of the market. The different ways of using your service level, quality and selection to differentiate your business are:

Convenience

The following are six categories of convenience:

- Location
- Delivery or Mobile Services
- Easy Ordering
- Availability
- Payment Terms
- Additional Services

Education or Training

Education and Training represent two of the most powerful value added services especially if you are selling a commodity type product or service where application knowledge is required.

The Best target market category

The best target market categories are your past and present customers. Your past and present customers who are the most neglected are usually the most productive of any and all target markets.

Your past and present customers have already bought from you so they already trust you; therefore, they are the easiest of the entire group to sell to.

Strategies for Segmenting Your List

After you have selected your target market, the next step in the process is finding ways of reaching them.

In the media section, we will address the various media through which you can channel your marketing message to your target audience.

In this section, I would like to quickly address the most popular channel which is: purchasing prospect list.

The most common way of reaching your target market is through direct response advertising through email, postal mail or placing an ad in specific publications.

In order to target your market, you need to be able to choose the right mailing list.

There are two types of mailing lists:

- Compiled list
- Response list

Compiled Lists

Compiled lists are generally cold prospects because the names and contact details have been gathered from various sources, such as survey companies, telemarketing firms and residential address databases.

A cold mailing list is one that contains contacts who have never heard of you, your business or your products or services. They have not expressed any interest or requested information. Since your business or products or services are not known to them, they are more difficult to generate sales from.

How to you obtain compiled lists?

A Compiled list can be obtained from various list brokers, trade organisations, magazines and libraries. You can also obtain compiled lists from other non-competing businesses in your area that serve the same market you are targeting.

For example a dentist could collect the list of the local golfing clubs.

If your product or service is for consumers, you could get a list of new homeowners in your area.

Acquiring the list of new homeowners in your area and communicating with them immediately is a very good way of getting customers. Research shows that 77% of consumers remain loyal to businesses that contact them first.

The following is the percentage of services new homeowners acquire:

- 70% will pick a new Dentist
- 74% (w/pets) a new Veterinarian
- 61% Hair Stylist
- 56% Auto Repair
- 33% Landscape/Lawn Care
- 65% Bank
- 17% Child Care

They also buy home improvement materials:

- Window Treatments 60%
- Furniture 62%
- Garden Centre 47%
- Carpeting/Tile/Flooring 55%
- Bedding/Linens 54%
- Telephone 28%
- Washer/Dryer 28%

Over 25% of new homebuyers are from out of town and another 25%-50% move from outside a 10-mile radius.

So you can see the enormous power of this list.

Imagine what will happen to a dental practice, if it constantly acquires the list of new comers to its town.

Here are three ways to obtain a newcomer list:

- Directly from the local recorder office
- From a local list company
- Telephone or utility companies

If your business caters to new businesses, you can obtain new business list from the company's house or local data companies.

Again, the goal here is to get in before your competitors contact them.

Response Lists

Response lists consist of information about people who have responded to an offer in some way.

These could be customers who have made recent purchases or prospects who have expressed an interest in specific products or services.

Customer lists are the most profitable type to have—either in electronic or traditional form—because it is easier to generate sales from people who have already made a purchase of your type of product or service.

Hot prospect lists are also valuable because these people have expressed a direct interest in your product or service.

Warm prospect lists may consist of people who have purchased similar or related products or services recently or have expressed an interest in related products or services.

Obviously, compiled lists are cheaper than response lists but in the long run, response lists always work out cheaper because they are more targeted and you know what type of purchases those on the list have made.

For example if you were selling marketing or business growth to lawyers, if you got a list of lawyers who have attended marketing or business growth seminars, you know they are more likely to be responsive to your offer.

Or if you were selling luxury products or services, instead of just finding a list of residents in a particular postcode, you could find a list of residents in that postcode who own a Ferrari or Bugatti.

You can afford to increase the sequence of your communication to them.

As we have seen, you cannot just send a single communication to your prospects and hope they will buy your product or service; in most instances, you will need a series of communications to persuade people to buy.

How to Calculate Your Cost Per Lead

In order to be in the position to communicate with your prospects multiple times, you need to know your cost per lead, to ensure you are not operating at a loss.

Let's say you pay £1,000 for a list that reaches 100,000 people, that divides out to just a penny each!

How many of those people never see your ad? Have no interest whatsoever, in your product or service; have brand name or current vendor loyalty?

But if you ran that as a lead generation ad, you could measure cost per lead, which is much more relevant than cost of circulation.

If you offered a free report in a weekly newspaper with 100,000 circulation, you might get 50 responses. If out of those 50 responses you get a six percent conversion rate, it will result in three clients.

Based upon the above calculation, your cost per lead will be £10.00 and your cost per customer acquisition will be £166.67.

If instead of placing the ad in a newspaper, you decided to conduct a mailing campaign, your cost per customer acquisition will be completely different.

I will illustrate this point using a hypothetical example based upon a six and nine percent conversion rate respectively.

In order to acquire a single client, you will require seventeen leads at a six percent conversion rate.

To get seventeen leads, you will need 185 names at a nine percent conversion rate.

185 names will cost you £18.52 at a cost of £100 per thousand names.

To convert those name into leads, you will need a three step follow-up marketing campaign (letter, phone call, email etc.) which will set you back by £277.78.

If you added £277.78 to £18.52, your total cost per customer acquisition will be £296.30.

To get your cost per lead, divide the £296.30 by the 17 leads, which means your cost per lead will be £17.

This is a template you could use to know your cost per customer acquisition and your cost per leads.

In the measuring your marketing results section of the book, I further drilled down into the customer acquisition calculation.

Essentials of a Good List

What should you look for if you decided to purchase a response list?

If you went to a list broker to purchase a response list, you need to know the following about the list in order to ensure a successful marketing campaign:

The source of the list: you need to know how the data on the list was gathered.

- Are they subscribers to a magazine?
- Did they purchase something?
- Did they respond to a space ad, TV or radio ad?

The Offer: what was the offer the people on the list responded to?

- Did they respond to a bill-me-later offer?
- Was it is premium purchase?
- Was there a coupon in the offer?

The price: What was the price of the offer they responded to:

- Was it a low price or premium price item they bought?
- How much money did they spend?

The mailing circle: how often was the list used?

- Has it been rented to other people in your niche or other niches?

Mail piece format:

What format was the mail they responded to sent in?

Was it:

- A letter
- Package
- Post card

Transactional vs updated information:
- Did the transactions happen that same month or were they several months old?

Frequency:
- How often do individuals on the list buy?

The universe:
- How often is the list tested?

The services bureau:
- Is the company that maintains the list credible?

Interest and affinity:
- What is your affinity with the list, can it relate to you?

Demographic:
- What is the age group on the list, gender or income etc.?

Usage: who else uses the list?
- How many companies have used the list successfully?

Respond and backend:
- What was the response to the usage of the list?

List cost:
- What is the cost of the list?

CPP Metrics:
- What is your cost per thousand?

Branding:
- The individuals on the list, have they heard about your company?

Benefit and experience:
- What experience have people on the list had with using your type of product and service?

Editorial philosophy:
- Is the list you are considering have a conservative or liberal philosophy?

List consumption preference:
- Does your product or service fit that list?
- Do individuals on the list like consuming your type of product or service in the manner you want to sell it to them?

Price & offer:
- Is your price and offer suitable for the list type?

List of High Leverage Prospects

It is essential that you narrow your segmentation to focus on the highest-level prospect in order to maximise your marketing resources.

The concept of high leverage prospects is relative and it differs from business to business.

The idea behind targeting high leverage prospects is to determine the path of least resistance, which will produce the greatest profit.

The four categories of high leverage prospects are:

1. The largest prospects
2. The smaller prospects
3. The neglected prospects
4. Market influencers

The Largest Prospects

The Largest Prospects are individuals or businesses that represent enormous profitability to your business.

There are two sides to the largest prospects coin: they represent very high turnover but less profit.

On the flip side of the coin, they represent enormous sources of credibility.

When you have famous companies on your books, it opens other doors for you.

However, servicing large prospects can be enormously demanding and risky.

They could swallow up all of your resources and if they represent a large portion of your business, if they got into trouble, it game over for you.

The Smaller Prospects

Smaller prospects have two sides of their coin as well.

They generally produce substantially higher profit margins, since they require less servicing.

In addition, their sales circle is pretty short.

Unlike larger prospects the smaller prospects might require a single visit.

On the other end of the coin, it is very expensive to market to them because they are difficult to reach.

The Neglected Prospects

These are the prospects that neglected by all of the businesses in the industry, because of size, location, costs or financial limitations. These could be in small towns and cities or very low income areas.

There are lots of professional services that will not open shop in low income areas because those resident in those areas cannot afford their services.

However, if you can find a way of enabling the residents to pay for your services, maybe through instalment payment or reduced service you could still make a killing in those areas.

Market Influencers

Market influencers are businesses and individuals who have strong credibility with your targeted prospects such as the chamber of commerce.

Workshop

1. Have you conducted a systematic process of identifying your target market?

_____

_____

_____

2. Have you segmented your market into different categories to enable you focus your marketing message and resources?

_____

_____

_____

3. What do you use as a lead magnet to incentivise your prospects to pay attention to your marketing message?

_____

_____

_____

4. Do you have a systematic referral system in place to create a pipeline of new prospects from your current customers?

_____

_____

_____

5. Do you have a system in place for upselling or cross selling your prospects and customers?

_____

_____

_____

6. Do you currently purchase mailing list? If so, which list do you purchase: complied or response list?

_____

_____

_____

7. If you sell Business to Business, do acquire list of newly formed businesses? If you sell business to consumer, do you acquire a list of new residence to your neighbourhood?

_____

_____

_____

8. Do you know your cost per customer acquisition?

_____

_____

_____

9. Have you identified your high leverage prospects and do you have a strategy in place to ensure you maximise your marketing return on investment?

_____

_____

_____

10. Do you have a strategy for courting market influencers such as your chamber of commerce, to allow them provide you market exposure?

_____

_____

_____

Your Marketing Media

The last few months I have attended a lot of different business shows and exhibitions.

Being a marketing consultant, as I walked around the stands I am constantly scanning for headlines and good taglines I could steal.

I visited stands and spoke to exhibitors hoping they were going to try selling me in order for me to learn their sales pitch.

However, almost without fail, I noticed many of the exhibitors just showed us a tick box exercise in order to convince themselves that they had done some form of marketing for the year.

And those exhibition stands are not particularly cheap. The smallest one could set you back about three thousand pounds (£3000).

As I went around, I kept thinking to myself, some entrepreneur has wasted £3000 of his hard earn money in order to make himself feel good that he has done some type of marketing.

For many of their staff members, it's an opportunity to get out of the office from the eyes of prying bosses or a chance to be seen to be doing something.

At least when it comes time for their appraisal, they could claim that they were the ones who did the presentation at the exhibition never mind the fact that they did not make a single sale.

Probably in nine out of ten of the stands, I had to go into the stands to ask what they did because it was not clear from their signs what the business they were into.

Some of them had the names of their companies in large lettering as if their companies were Coca Cola or Nike.

Some of them even paid for workshop and presentation slots only to hire presenters who did not bother to read their script before the presentation to familiarise themselves with the presentation prior to the event.

But those were not like the main things I observed.

The main thing that really surprised me was not a single person tried selling me anything.

They were all concerned with collecting my details and promising to contact after the show instead of trying to close me right there and then.

I am sure there were lots of people like me who would have bought something if they felt it was valuable to them.

However, because no one tried to sell anything, many of the exhibitors went home empty handed.

So why did many of those companies including some really big players make such a colossal error?

There are two answers to this question.

The first is this: for many businesses, marketing means placing an ad in newspapers, on radio, in the yellow pages or exhibiting at a business show.

Secondly, not a lot of businesses follow the steps we have followed above: to first craft their marketing message, identify their target market before considering the media through which to channel their marketing message.

Marketing media such as newspapers, magazines, TV, radio or social media are just conduits through which to channel your marketing message.

Placing the wrong marketing massage in front of the wrong audience is a waste of resources.

Equally so, placing a great marketing message in the wrong media is a waste of resources.

What do I mean by this?

Let's say your target market is professionals: dentists, lawyers, accountants or medical doctors.

To place your ads in Facebook or buy space in sport magazine is a waste of money.

Yes, there are many of those professionals on Facebook and many of them read sports magazines.

However, the layers of unqualified prospects you have to go through on Facebook or a sports magazine to reach any of those professionals will not be worth your time and effort.

Chances are you might probably run out of money before getting a handful of them.

On the other hand, if you were to place the same ad in a trade magazine for those professions or place your ad on LinkedIn, your chances of reaching them is pretty high.

Furthermore, when you are placing the ad on Facebook or a sports magazine, you will have to dilute the message to appeal to a wide audience.

But if you were targeting the same professionals in their trade magazines, you could tailor the marketing message to suit them. This is the reason why the three-step process is very important.

If you want to run a successful marketing campaign, you will need to follow the steps as I have outlined them in this training:

1. Craft an effective marketing message
2. Identify your target mark
3. Select the right media through which to channel the marketing message.

In some instances, you could change the order of steps one and two.

You could spot a market or opportunity and determine you are in the position to fill that gap so you an effective marketing message to appeal to that market.

However, for businesses that are already in existence and are seeking to attract more customers, since you already know what you are selling, all you need to do is craft an effective marketing message, select a segment of your market and select the right media through which to channel that marketing message.

The Various Types of Marketing Media

What are the various types of marketing media?

There are:

Offline media:

- Newspapers & Magazines
- TV & Radio
- Billboard
- Events
- Product giveaway
- Discount coupons
- Postal and leaflets
- Direct mail

Online media

- Social media
- Your website
- Blog
- Pop Ups
- Banner ad
- Video sites
- Article directories

By today's standard, many of the offline media have become expensive.

We are becoming accustom to free things.

Social media one of the most powerful marketing tools of our generation is sort of free and these days anyone could build a website for free.

There is a good and a bad news, because of this phenomenon.

The good news is the barrier to entry into any business has been lowered considerably.

Anyone can wake up in the middle of the night, think of a business idea; launch the business right on the spot…Well sort of.

I said sort of, because anyone who puts up a website can now claim to be in business. Never mind that he could not have a single customer or any valuable product or service to sell.

Never the less it's a good news for anyone with the ability to take advantage of the ease with which things can be done these days.

The bad news is competition is becoming steeper. Well sort off, almost every industry is coming overcrowded.

Even services that were once owned by a handful of professionals with the resources to establish their own business are slowly becoming overcrowded as many professionals flock to establish their own businesses because they feel all they need to market their professional firms is a website and social media account.

An accountant will obtain his CPA, instead of searching for work, he will open his own accounting firm because he is under the illusion that all he needs is a website and a Facebook page and his phone will never stop ringing with clients begging for his services.

Only for him to rent an office and register the company before realising the error he has made. First of all, a proper business is not about having a website site, a business needs a proper infrastructure to be considered a business.

Even online businesses do not just operate online; the most successful ones have offline infrastructures.

Many people are under the illusion that marketing has become cheap because of the internet.

I hate to be the one breaking this news to you, but marketing has become more expensive than it has ever been. The main reason for this is the lowering of the barrier to entry.

While the internet has created opportunity for more people than ever to establish their own business, it has also made it more difficult to reach customers.

People are overwhelmed with marketing messages bombarding them from different directions.

The average person is exposed to over three thousand advertising messages a day and that continues to increase. This does not even include popup banners and ads on social media.

Therefore, people are doing their best to avoid any message that smells like an ad. For this reason, instead of the internet making it less expensive to reach people, it has become more expensive.

It does not matter what media you choose to use, online or offline, the cost of reaching prospects is continuously skyrocketing.

Even with the skyrocketing cost, there is no guarantee that because you spend a fortune on your ad, you will reach your target.

As I have pointed out in the first instance, they are already overwhelmed with advertising messages coming at them from different directions.

Secondly, you will think that with the iPhones and iPads that make it easy for people to get things done, they will have time to spare.

What the iPhones, iPads, social media and all the other gadgets have done is take away people's ability and desire to concentrate on any single thing for long.

What your marketing message is competing with is someone filming himself drinking a gallon of vodka in one go. Free porn and women big boobs freely available on YouTube.

So your prospect is a young lawyer or doctor who has been working a twelve-hour shift. What do you think will be more interesting to him, watching girl with big boobs on YouTube or reading your sales letter?

That's for you to decide.

All I am telling you is, we are living in the attention deficit age where a lot and lots of different things are vying for your prospects attention.

This is why if you intend on getting through to them, you need to be strategic.

If you approached your marketing as most businesses do, you will struggle to reach your prospects.

Challenges Facing Your Marketing Message

The first challenge you face when you send your marketing message is, will it to be opened? Most people have spam filter that filters their emails.

Any message considered spam is sent immediately to the junk folder.

If your message manages to survive the spam filter, the second challenge is, is it enticing enough to get your prospect to open it?

This is where most of the stuff we have discussed in the previous sections come into play.

To get someone to open an email from someone he/she does not know; your subject line has to be captivating.

You will not be unable to write a captivating subject line that speaks directly to your target audience if you do not understand their thought process or know who they are.

If by some luck of the draw, you manage to pass challenge number two – he opens your email; your headline and introduction had better be able to captivate his attention in the first few seconds.

He is not going to sit there get a coffee and start reading your email, he is going to scan. Therefore, you need to ensure your email is well written and structured to stop him in his tracks and force him to read it.

By the way, similar a process applies to postal delivery mail.

Legendary copywriter Gary Halbert once said people sort their mail over the wastebasket. Any mail that has the slightest resemblance of an ad is dumped in the wastebasket.

So the question now is: how do you prevent your ad from looking like an ad?

I need you to pay serious attention to this answer because this is a very critical point in your marketing…

If your ad is not open or read, it does not matter how good the message is and it does not matter if it is the right target audience, it will not be acted upon which is why it is very crucial you pay your undivided attention to this point.

In order to ensure your ad escapes being tossed into the wastebasket, you need to make the *ad itself appear valuable*.

What do I mean by that?

Just look at some marketing brochures you recently received. If you still have any at home. How do they look to you? What do they signal to you? Many of them immediately signal someone is trying to sell you something.

Some might look glossy, colourful and expensive, that for many businesses; constitutes value. Value does not mean an expensive looking brochure.

Let me explain what I mean by make your ad look valuable….When I say make your marketing material look valuable, what I mean is your ad needs to look like something that will give them something not take away from them.

Your ad needs to look like it is something that will give them valuable information when they read it.

Your ad should not read sales all over it.

Let me stick to offline media for now but we will address a similar thing when we deal with online media.

When you want to send out an ad, you need to pay careful attention to the format in which it is going to be sent. If you are sending out an envelope, you need to ensure the envelope itself looks valuable.

There are certain envelopes you will send a letter in that will prompt your prospect to open and there are envelopes you will use that will prompt your prospect to toss your marketing message into the waste basket.

This comes down to the technique of addressing the envelope and stuff, which we are not going to be addressing in this workbook.

However, be aware that if you do not want your marketing message ending up in the wastebasket, you need to ensure it appears valuable.

Another way of preventing your marketing message from ending up in the waste basket is to use special delivery.

This brings up another dimension in your marketing process that is to know the value of each customer to you.

Many businesses ignore the importance of knowing their numbers but knowing your numbers is the core element in the success of any business. There is no way a business will become profitable if top management do not know certain numbers.

Two of the most important numbers a business needs to know are:

- The cost of your customer acquisition
- The value of each customer to your business

One reason knowing the value of each customer to you is important is, it will allow you to determine the amount you are willing to spend to acquire customers.

Let me make this point and if there is just one thing you get from this entire workbook, let it be this: sales and marketing is buying customers.

Do not delude yourself that you are going to build a business empire for free.

Case Study

I always have this discussion with business owners when they come to me to help them with their marketing.

My first question is; where do you want to be twelve months from now?

They will explain to me about the emotions they will like to feel. Then I will say, I need figures, I know money is not the only outcome but we need something we can count.

Probably after quizzing them for a few minutes, they will come up with some figure.

My next question is how much resources do you have at your disposal to achieve that figure?

Most of the times it is zip…nada…zero…

I remember having a conversation with someone who told me she wanted to make a quarter of a million in twelve months' time.

I said to her, 'do you know that in order for you to make a quarter of a million you will need a marketing budget of at least thirty thousand; I will suggest fifty thousand to be on the safe side.

Your current internal infrastructure, your current skill level and your current talent in your organisation cannot take you from less than a hundred thousand to a quarter of a million; it is not possible. You need to strengthen your infrastructure if you want to achieve that level of income. She looked at me as if I was speaking Greek.

At the beginning, I spoke about the failure of 75% of start-up businesses.

The main reason the majority of businesses fail is they run out of cash.

Motivational gurus, coaches and some business consultants talk about passion and belief.

It's good to be passionate about what you are doing, it's good to have belief in yourself but it's also good to have the ability to take the necessary actions to achieve your goal.

Except you developed some type of whiz bag software or app, there is no way anyone is going to mathematically move a business from twenty thousand pound to a quarter of a million pounds in a year without a major cash injection. It will never happen.

I know I am going on a tantrum here moving away from the topic but I wanted to stress the point that marketing is about buying customer.

If you do not have the ability or the willingness to buy customers, you might as well stop reading this workbook because it is not going to help you.

The large majority of business owners do not want to spend a single red penny on marketing or many want to spend the least amount possible yet expect a massive return on investment.

Like any natural law, you get out what you put in. If you put in peanuts, you will receive peanuts in return.

Here is another thing you might want to highlight.

Ideally, what you want to do is put yourself in the position where you are able to spend more on your marketing than your competitors.

That should be your goal with your marketing, to put yourself in the position where you are capable of spending ten times as much on your marketing than your closet competitor.

The reason companies like Nike, Coca Cola or McDonald remain the leader in their field even though they are constantly facing steep competition is they are willing and capable of outspending all of their competitors combined, more than a thousand times.

Pepsi have been trying for years to eat into the Coke market, they have still not been able to as much as scratch the surface of the coke market share because coke is willing and capable of outspending them by billions.

Can you imagine the amount of sportswear companies that have been trying hard to steal market share from Nike?

Have they even been able to get anywhere close to Nike?

No way. Nike is outspending all of them combined by billions.

What am I saying here? I am not saying you need to have billions to spend on your marketing; what I am saying is you need *to understand that you are not going to build your business empire for free.*

You will have to deploy some resources if you want to achieve your goals or you will remain in the same position and someday when another person willing to spend for their marketing enters your niche, you will be history.

The reason I have gone off on the tantrum is just to make the point that there are times when you will need to pay for special delivery in order to ensure your message is opened.

Your message cannot be read if it is not opened so we need to give yourself the best chance of it been opened.

No one, absolutely no one ever throws out a FedEx or UPS.

Can you imagine someone receiving a FedEx or UPS parcel and tossing it in the wastebasket? It will never happen.

I spoke about knowing the value of your customer.

One of the reasons for that is I will not expect you to send all of your marketing messages to all of your prospects using FedEx or UPS.

However, if you knew that a customer has a high value to you, you should be willing to do whatever it takes to ensure your message reaches them.

I only used FedEx and UPS as examples because everyone knows them. There are other less expensive ways you could reach your prospect but they need to be ways that ensure your message is opened.

What Next After It Is Opened?

Getting your message opened is the first step in the process.

You breeze pass that hurdle, now, what next?

The next step in the process is what happens when the target opens the envelope.

Like an email, you only have a few seconds to capture his/her attention.

Simply because you pay for special delivery does not mean that your message is read. The special delivery only guarantees it is opened.

When is it opened, you need to give the target a reason to read it.

The only reason they will read it is, if it does not look like ad to them.

Case Study

Let me use our own sales process to illustrate this point better.

We serve different niches, so I will use our retail program as an example.

We have a retail home study course called 'How to Increase Retail Sales'.

I have written a book called 'How to Increase Retail Sales'.

And we have a leaflet entitled 'How to Increase Retail Sales'.

If we wanted to attract a retail client, which one of the three will we use?

The answer is, it depends.

If we wanted to land Marks & Spencer, Next or John Lewis, we are not going to send their CEO the book or the leaflet.

We will send them the home study course plus the book. And we will use special delivery because we know any of those accounts will land us millions.

However, if we were sending the same information to a smaller retailer, again depending on how valuable we perceive them to be, we will send the home study course or the book.

We use the leaflet in circumstances where we have no chance of accessing the prospect and we just wanted to leave information.

Like if I attended a retail event and I had no means of discussing with many of the people at the event, I will locate our leaflet at strategic locations of the venue where I am sure it will be seen.

But here is the point.

If we wanted to pass the open test with a retailer, we will send the book or home study course by special delivery.

There is no retailer in the world who will open an envelope, see a book or home study course that says 'How to Increase Retail Sale' who will throw it away.

No retailer will ever think of doing that.

We have books and home study courses for all of our different niches: law, accounting, dental practice, restaurant or private medical practice.

So when we want to target those niches, we send out either the books or home study course depending on the value we place on the prospect.

They always lead to business if not on the spot; they lead to business in the future.

Therefore, we know if we sent out hundred and got one business out of it, we would have broken even.

If we got five businesses out of it, we will be in massive profit.

But the point I am trying to make here is:

> One – I ensure our marketing message is opened
> Two – I ensure it is read

My book or home study course at this point is the marketing message.

What If They Do Not Respond

Your message managed to pass the open test and they read it.

What if they do not take action immediately, what do you do?

This brings us to the third step in the process, which is the follow-up sequence.

You cannot be arrogant to think that the moment prospective clients receive your marketing material, because it is valuable, they will drop everything and read it.

And after reading it, they will take whatever action you wish them to take.

To think in that manner is naive.

As I said previously, people are busy; they have their iPhone, iPad and blackberry to look at.

They have work to do, family to attend to and least I forget chic boobs to watch on YouTube.

Your marketing message is the least of their worries.

It might be a few minutes after receiving your message, when the euphoria of receiving a parcel dies down, they have already forgotten about it. The euphoria of receiving a parcel will wear off in ten minutes time and they will be back to where they started.

Secondly, even if they read you message, they might not have a need for your service at that point in time.

They might not have money…

They might have another supplier…

Their brother-in-law might be their vendor and they do not want to upset him.

There are whole raft of reasons that might prevent them from taking action on your message at that point even though they find it very valuable.

This is why the third step in the process, the follow-up sequence is very essential.

Getting qualified prospects to at least read or listen to your offer, and ultimately to become customers, requires repetition.

Repetition to the masses is very expensive; this is why it is necessary you market to only your target prospects to ensure you can afford repetition.

When I mean repetition, I am not suggesting you send out book or home study course multiple times although that will be the most effective but it will be very expensive.

What I am suggesting is, in the first instant you send something valuable. It could be a books or home study course as we do…

If you do not have either of those, depending on your type of business, you could send a letter directing them to a website where they will be able to download a free report… although this is not a very effective method, if you do not have a book; this will suffice.

After you have sent the first valuable stuff, you could follow it up with another valuable stuff a letter or a post card.

Then you can follow it up with a phone call, then another phone call and an email.

Here is the thinking behind this process. The goal is not to become a pest that just keeps sending them junk in the name of following up.

You need to be tactical about the process and respectful of the other person.

There are basically four things you want to achieve in your communication with your prospects.

- You must get them to read or listen to your proposition
- You must get them to understand the benefits of your product or service
- You must get them to have confidence in your company's ability to fulfil the promised benefit
- You must motivate them to take action

You will not achieve any of the above by irritating them.

You will only achieve it by being very tactical in your communication.

You cannot send the send information to them every single time; it will be classed as junk or sperm.

Every time you communicate with them, the goal has to be to leave them better than they were when they received your communication.

This is one of the reasons why every business should have a newsletter so that in the worst case scenario, you can send them your monthly newsletter.

But your follow-up process has to be systematic, deliberate, tactical and above all valuable to your prospects.

The caveat here is what you use as your initial lead magnet and follow-up sequence will depend upon your industry and your type of business.

Website

As a business, your websites have become the predominant means of delivering your marketing message.

In fact, for most businesses their website is the only means through which they deliver their marketing message. For many people what they consider their business is their website.

There are millions of people whose business as they will describe it, is their website.

This section is not meant to address anyone with a so-called online business (someone with just a website).

It is meant for businesses with proper infrastructure that use their website as a lead generation magnet to drive traffic to their business.

There are three types of websites:

- Brochure website
- E-commerce website
- Lead generation website

The common denominator that runs through all three is:

- Traffic generation
- Traffic conversion

What the majority of businesses have are brochure websites, they hope will work for them as a lead generation magnet.

Let me quickly describe the three in order for you to understand the distinctions.

A brochure website as the name implies, is a brochure that only tells visitors about you and your business.

These are usually websites of large corporate organisations staffed by people with little or no marketing knowledge or, organisations that feel they have no reason to sell themselves.

However, many small businesses have adopted the corporate look on their websites without understanding the reason behind large corporation having that type of website.

I always have this discussion with my prospects or clients.

When I receive call from businesses that want me to help them with their marketing, the first thing I do is check out their website.

After going through their website, I usually advise we make some changes to it to make it fit for purpose.

Most of the times, this suggestion ends up becoming big debates because for them a website needs to look fancy with lots of bells and whistles. They do not understand that a website is about functionality.

The second type of website is an e-commerce website. The goal of an ecommerce website is basically to be used as an online store.

The third type of website is a lead generation website. Lead generation websites as the name implies is for generating leads.

This is the most appropriate type of website the majority of businesses need.

In fact, every business needs to have a lead generation website even if it has a brochure website to satisfy the guys at the head office.

A lead generation website has a single goal: to attract leads that later become customers.

Ninety-nine percent of businesses with websites are not achieving the goal for which they build their websites.

There are two reasons for this:

- Firstly, many businesses did not construct their websites with any objective.
- Secondly, many businesses do not even know that their websites need to be constructed with a specific objective

Many businesses have their website designed by designers who know nothing about marketing. Designers who know design but do not know marketing therefore, do not construct the site with the objective of attracting customers.

Your website has to be incorporated into your overall marketing strategy, which means it needs to be functional.

I have a Bulgarian friend who is an architect. When he draws a building, he draws the building the way it will look when it is occupied.

If it is a residential property, all of the rooms will be occupied, there will be people sleeping in the bedrooms, bathing in the bathroom, eating in the dining room or sitting in the lounge.

I asked why he drew his buildings that way; he responded 'architecture is about functionality.'

The building is being constructed for a specific reason. It is either a residential or a business premises. Whatever the purpose for which the building is being constructed its function has to be taken into account.

The same principle has to be applied to your website construction. You need to construct your website to take into account the reason for which it is been constructed.

Since it is obvious that the majority of businesses construct their website to generate leads, it goes without saying that the website has to be constructed in a specific way to facilitate the generation of leads.

Your website as a lead generation magnet needs to be focused on two things:

- Good marketing messages that speak directly to you target prospects
- Functionality

Don't panic I am not going to go all technical on you. My goal in this section is to provide you the fundamentals of a website to provide you the requisite information to speak to your technical person rationally. You will also possess the competence to ask the questions and to know what result to expect.

When it comes to your website, the keyword I like you to always keep at the top of your mind is *user experience*.

What is the user experience of your website?

Just think about it in this manner.

Let say you ran a retail store and someone came into your store, you expect them to find what they are looking for easily right?

If they had to struggle to find what they are looking for, do you think they will remain in your store, or will they ever return? The same principle applies to any business.

If you had an office in the middle no nowhere, causing visitors to struggle to locate it, how many people you imagine will want to go through the hassle of finding your office?

The same principle applies to your website. When people visit your website, they are there for a particular reason; if they do not find what they are looking for the moment they click on your website, they are gone. You do not get to have a second chance.

Critical Questions about Your Website

You need to be able to answer the following three questions about your website:

- Who am I trying to persuade?
- What action do I want them to take?
- What action do they want to take?

Your design structure needs to leave them in no doubt what you want them to do

You can see from the first question, it boils down to what we have been discussing all through this workbook: your marketing message and your target market.

When you arrive at my website there is no doubt that my target market are small business owners. It is there written in black and white. But it is also speaking to a specific type of small business owner, the one who wants to attract customers, needs business or wants to create marketing plan.

It is also evident what I like them to do: fill in my opt-in form because I want to capture their details.

As a reward for giving me their details, they will receive a business growth report. Plus they can sign up for a free business growth and marketing consultation.

If you went to any of my lead generation pages, you will notice I follow similar pattern:

- This is what I have
- This is what it will do for you
- This is why I am doing it
- This is what I would like you to do

Functionality and User Experience

Another element of the websites are *functionality* and *user experience*.

There is a big difference between functionality and user experience.

> *Functionality answers the question: Does your website do what it was constructed for? i.e. capture leads, sell products or sell your services.*

User experience answers the question: can the user easily find what they are looking for?

This is a very crucial point:

> There is what you want the website to do
>
> And
>
> There is what the user wants from your website.

There is a thin line between your desire and the users' desire. The genius comes from your ability to merge your wants with your user desire.

Conversion the Critical Element of Website

This brings us to the second critical part of any website: conversion.

I touched upon conversion in the section on functionality, usability and customer experience.

Conversion is simply getting visitors to take the action you like them to take when they arrive on your site.

To get them to take the action you want them to take, your marketing message has to appeal to them and the website has to be designed to make it possible for them to take the action you like them to take.

What I really want to discuss in terms of conversion is the structure of your sales/marketing funnel.

Your sales/marketing funnel is your customer buying process – the steps your prospects need to go through to buy from you. This goes back to ease of doing business with your – customer experience.

When someone fills up the form on your website, how easy is it for him/her to download the information you promised. When they pay for products, how easy it is for them to download their purchase or receive confirmation of purchase?

If it is only about them setting appointment for free consultation, how easy is it for them to fill up the form.

***I am using the words sales and marketing here interchangeably to simplify the explanation.

Your Marketing Funnel

First part of the funnel:

Whether it is online, or offline, the biggest barrier to sales is trust. Trust is the key to whether a business transaction reaches a satisfactory conclusion for both parties.

Firstly, many people have been burned by legitimate businesses that do not keep their promise.

Customer service is at an all-time low. People go to what are legitimate businesses: retail stores, restaurants or their neighbourhood dry cleaners and they return with catalogue of bad experiences. What do you think their level of scepticism is when dealing with someone they have never met?

> *They have not been to your place of business, for all they know you might not even exist except on the web.*

Consequently, the question you need to answer constantly in your website presentation and marketing message, is **have you made an effort through your website design, presentation and message to increase credibility and decrease scepticism?**

The more credible you appear in terms of your message and presentation, the easier it will be for them to do business with you. Trust is the keyword here; they need to trust you.

Second part of the funnel:

The second thing is how easy is it for them to receive what they sign up or paid for.

Third part of the funnel:

Thirdly, what is your after sales process? A sale in this context does not necessarily mean monetary sales. I mean after they have taken the action you wanted them to take, what happens next?

If they sign up to watch your video or download your report, after reading the report, what happens next?

Conversion is Difficult

The first thing I will say about conversion is this: Never, never, underestimate the difficulty of getting someone to put their hands in their wallet and give you their money.

Whether you are selling on the internet or face-to-face, you will be aware of the fact that the majority of times, the sale process collapses at the point of sales because this is where people begin to have second thoughts.

If you are selling bread, sugar or milk and you are the only off license in town, then you need not worry about conversion.

However, if you are in any other business, know that it is difficult to get another human being to part with their money.

The reason many businesses lose the sale at this point is they do not give this part of the sale process the level of seriousness it requires.

In this case, we are dealing with conversion in the context of your website. However, it is important that you understand that you need a good conversion process in every spectrum of your business, whether it's on the web or during face to face transaction.

> *What I am about to teach you is a very powerful stuff so I must caution not to use it for evil because you will end up in marketing hell.*

I am not about to teach you trickery or tactics used by unscrupulous sale people to persuade people to take decisions that are not in their best interest.

I am talking about conscientiously holding your prospects hand and helping them make decisions that are in their best interest not decisions that are bad for them. However, you persuading them to take certain decisions simply because you want to make quick profit out of them.

You will not get rich like that and I promise you, you will end up in marketing hell if you use this information for evil.

Conversion is what has made Amazon the most dominant retailer in the world today. Online retailers such as Amazon and eBay have hundreds of staff sat in their office watching the activities of every visitor to their sites.

Based upon the data they collect, they keep tweaking their site design to serve their visitors in the continuous effort of increasing conversion.

Recently, I attended a retail technology exhibition; one of the most popular technologies at the event was customer tracking.

These are technologies used to track the activities of customers in real time in retail stores.

These are the types of technologies being used by the most successful retailers because they understand the benefit of knowing your customers.

They understand that knowing your customers is the only way to increasing conversion.

Marketing Funnel Checklist Point One

The first critical point about conversion that I need you to know is *never design your marketing funnel around your technology; it needs to be the other way around. You need to design your conversion technology around your marketing funnel.*

Let me just stop and define a marketing funnel. I do not want to make the false assumption that everyone reading this workbook understands what a marketing funnel is.

Your marketing funnel is simply the steps your prospects need to take before they finally purchase your product or service.

In the corporate world it is called buying circle. From the moment, they see your ad or sales letter or the moment they arrive on your website to the time they place the order, that space of time between coming into contact with your marketing information and taking your desired action is called: your marketing funnel.

What you have with most small businesses, they hire tech guys to create a marketing system for them that they lack the technical knowhow or the resources to effectively utilise.

So whatever system you decide to design has to account for your current resources and technical capabilities.

Marketing Funnel Checklist Point Two

The second critical point you need to take into consideration is:

- The length of your marketing funnel will depend on the extent of beliefs you need to establish in your prospects before they buy from you
- The complexity of the product or service
- The offer you are presenting them

When we go into the section on traffic generation, I will discuss in further detail the sequence of events required to drive traffic to your website but to further expand on this point, I will briefly touch on the traffic generation process here.

Let's say you buy traffic from google adwords. Someone clicks on your ad on google, it takes them to what is called a landing page (landing page is the page the Google ad is linked to).

Clicking on the ad is the first step in your sales process.

When they land on your landing page, there is an action you want them to take, that action is the second step in the process.

Let's say when they land on the page you gave them a free report or an instructional video; that is the second step in the process.

After watching the video, you expect them to take a certain action, that action is the third step in the process.

Now depending on the complexity of your product/service or offer, at this point you could ask them to buy or offer them another free thing.

After the third step, you could decide to offer them your product or service straight away, sell them a basic version and then sell them the deluxe version later or go straight for the kill here and sell them the deluxe version of your product or service.

So this is where conversion comes into place because at this point you need to test various strategies or sales funnels.

Here are two things you need to pay attention to – What happens when they arrive on your website and what happens afterwards.

Case Study

I am going to use our own business as an example to further drum down the concept of conversion.

Our deluxe product or service is coaching and consulting.

No one, not even Barack Obama with his ability to sell will be able to sell a thirty thousand pound coaching program online.

You could hire the best copywriters in the world, they will not succeed in convincing anyone to cough out thirty thousand pounds because of some brilliantly written sales letter on your website that promises the best consulting the world have ever seen – it is never going to happen.

Except the prospect or prospects already know us and have a relationship with us, we will not be able to convince them to part with their thirty thousand pounds.

The price of a product is never determined by the cost of bringing that product to the market as we have been taught all along, it is determined by who is buying and how it is sold to them.

How you market your product or service will determine who you can attract and the price you will be able to sell it for.

So what we do in our case is stair step the process.

We place what we call lead generation ads on google, Facebook and LinkedIn for a free video or free strategy session.

When someone clicks on the ad, it takes them to our landing page; by the way, we have different landing pages that we test regularly.

They get to the landing page and we ask them to download a free business growth report.

When they do that, at the bottom of the report, we sell them a book.

If they purchase the book, on the thank you page of the book, we sell them our home study course.

On the thank you page of the home study course, we offer them either free strategy session or workshop.

It is during the free strategy session or workshop we sell the coaching and consulting.

You could see our sales funnel is a series of steps. We can use three, four or five steps depending on the niche we are dealing with.

Certain niches require lots of convincing and other are simple to convince.

How do we determine the steps, marketing message and landing page design

This is where our conversion process comes into to play.

We have a software that track the activities of every single visitor to our site.

We sit and painstakingly go through each visitor's activities, their eyes and mouse movement.

We also test different types of headlines, sub-headlines, sales message, images, and video.

Based on the percentage of conversion we get after each test, we keep tweaking and changing things.

When it comes to conversion, it is the little things that make the difference. You need to have the ability to test and monitor the activities of visitors to your site.

The reason most website never convert traffic is, once it is built, it is fait accompli. The owner never optimise it for conversion.

Your website needs to be dynamic; it cannot be static.

As you read this, think of the last time, you made any type of changes on your website.

I am sure many of you will admit you have never touched your website since the time the designer gave it to them.

Don't you clean your office?

Has it not been cleaned since you moved into it?

Your website is like your office, if you like it to serve the purpose for which it was built, effectively, it needs to be cleaned regularly.

Lead Generation

Ideally, this section should have been the second part of the process of using your website as an effective marketing tool. You:

- Construct your website
- Drive traffic to it
- And then convert the traffic

However, because this is a marketing course, I have decided we first need to construct the website, put in mechanism for conversion and then we consider ways of driving traffic to it.

What I am going to discuss regarding traffic goes totally, against what many of you have either been taught or told about traffic generation.

There are two ways of driving traffic to your website:

- Free traffic
- Paid traffic

Free traffic as the phrase implies is traffic obtained from other sources for free.

It is traffic from social media, blogs, forums, articles, article directories, directories or links from other sites.

Paid traffic is traffic from Google, Bing, other search engines and social media sites.

Getting free traffic requires lots of search engine optimisation (SEO) work i.e. using the right keywords, constantly posting content on social media, article directories, forums, blogs and directories.

The majority of us small business owners build our websites and never attempt to drive traffic to it in any form whatever.

We believe that the fact that we have a website someone searching for our products or services will find us.

The few who are smart enough to know that they need traffic focus most of their attention of free traffic.

Let me drop the bombshell. The concept of free traffic is a myth.

Yes, you heard me right. I said the concept of free traffic is a myth.

There is nothing like free traffic. Free is those words use by online marketers to extract money from people who like freebie.

Free online traffic is like paying to sleep in a homeless shelter or buying food at the food bank.

It is a homeless shelter because you are supposed to be given shelter for a night without you having to cough-up money from your pocket.

It's the same with a food bank; it is for people who cannot afford to buy food.

Because those services are for people who cannot afford to pay for them, they are not only free, they are located in areas that are easily accessible to people who need them.

Contrast that with so-called free traffic.

Doing proper SEO for a website to remotely have a chance of appearing on the first page of google, (not even the first spot) will take three to six month.

YES three to six months for your website to have the remote chance of showing up in google search results.

Imagine as small business owner you are trying to drive traffic to your website, posting on social media, forums, blog, article directories, and all the rest; do you know how much time that will take you?

If you cannot afford to do it yourself, which is the situation with many small business owners, you have to pay someone to do it.

So how free is the traffic if you have to spend hours of your time each day for three to six months or pay someone to carry on the necessary activities for you?

The majority of companies on the first page are either insignificant companies, that got there by default because their sites have been up and running for a long time or they pay for the privilege.

So if there is no free traffic, what will I advise small business owners to do if they want to get traffic to their website?

I will advise you get paid traffic in the first instance.

You can use a mixture of both so-called free as well as paid traffic.

However, if you want customers like yesterday and you are hoping that you will attract customers to your site by posting on social media, forum or article directories, my condolences.

It will cost you more trying to get the so-called free traffic than you will spend on paid traffic.

The return of investment on paid traffic is so high these days that wasting time trying to drive free traffic to your website is treason.

Social Media

As I was writing this manuscript, it was announced that the Turkish government had blocked Twitter and YouTube.

Social media was wildly credited with fuelling the Arab spring and removing Arab strongmen who had been in power for years.

The election of President Barack Obama was attributed to his campaign team's effective use of social media.

Social media has also been responsible for some pretty negative things like the London riot, binge drinking and cyber bullying.

Following on from all of the above, social media is now considered by most businesses as an effective marketing tool.

Social media is indeed an effective marketing tool if and only if you have the ability and the willingness to pay for it.

Like the myth about free website traffic, free social media for business is a myth.

Collectively the social media sites have over two billon followers.

Facebook alone has close to a billion people.

Therefore, there is possibility that you will find your targeted prospect on one of the platforms.

Effective use of social media comes down to the other fundamentals we have spoken about in the other sections selecting the right target market and crafting a strong marketing message.

But, this is a big but.

To imagine you are going to post stuff on social media for free and build your business from it is an illusion.

I have had training from the twenty top online marketers in the world.

Not even one of those guys ever teaches social media as a source for generating traffic.

Paid traffic yes, but not free traffic.

The only one of them who taught social media as a source of free traffic was Don Crowther, but guess what, that was his niche. That was how he made his money.

However, he realised that people were catching up to him, he quickly changed to another niche.

Like Don, the only people who make money from free from social media are those who teach it.

The irony is this, even those who teach free social media for business, pay for the traffic to advertise their training. They do not post free on social media and expect people to attend their training.

I know a Facebook trainer who spends thousands of dollars per month to advertise her Facebook training in which she shows businesses how to get Facebook traffic to their website without spending a penny.

Can you imagine the irony in that?

She uses paid ads to teach people how to get free traffic from Facebook. If she knew how to get free traffic, why would she pay for it?

I am sure, when you saw social media in the sales letter of this workbook, you were expecting me to show you a thousand and one ways of getting free traffic from social media.

If you were running a political campaign like president Obama, or you were trying to remove your government from power, I could show you how to use social media for free to do that.

But trust me on this one: there is absolutely no business, I repeat no business that is growing their customer base as a result of free social media traffic.

If that were the case, the best online marketers who are making hundreds of millions from the internet would be using it.

I am really sorry if I disappointed you.

I am trying to save you months if not years of wasted time and resources trying to get free social media traffic.

This course is not aimed at teaching you how to drive paid traffic. It is more of a kind of technical stuff.

There are lots of training courses on driving paid social media traffic you can easily acquire.

How to Measure Your Marketing Results

Dan Kennedy one of the greatest marketers who ever graced the planet earth once said:

Marketing is psychology and mathematics.

The psychological aspect of marketing is understanding people's emotion because as we pointed out earlier, most human activities are based upon emotion.

People buy emotionally but justify their decisions logically.

Therefore, there is one keyword you should never forget when trying to market your product or service; that word is compassion… understanding the wants and desires of another human being.

Daniel Goldman the author of 'Emotional Intelligent' said there are three different types of ways to sense the other person's feeling:

The first is "cognitive empathy," commonly known as perspective taking. This is simply knowing how the other person feels and what they might be thinking.

There's "emotional empathy," – when you feel physically along with the other person, as though their emotions were contagious.

Then there's "compassionate empathy," or "empathic concern". With compassionate empathy, we not only understand a person's predicament and feel with them, we are spontaneously moved to help, if needed.

Effective marketing is about compassionate empathy – when we are moved to help the other person.

We must understand that despite our best intention, the other person might not necessarily feel or think that we are acting in their best interest. Because they themselves might not even know what is in their best interest or they might have been taken advantage of previously. That person is therefore naturally sceptical about anyone purporting to work in their interest, especially salespeople.

This is why we need to use different types of persuasive tools.

It's like trying to feed a child who does not want to eat. Of course as a parent trying to feed the child, you are working in its interest but the child does not view your attempt to feed it as something in its interest.

Like children, adults also need to be coaxed into taking their medications sometimes.

So when you are designing your marketing, you need to put yourself in the frame of mind that you are helping a child to eat or an adult to take his medication because it is in their interest in the long run.

The three most effective psychological marketing tools are:

- Star
- Story
- Solution

Your Need a Star

In the previous section, I said you needed to patronise your prospects.

The conventional wisdom is people don't like being patronised. But the reality is people do like being patronised. People like being led, which is why they look up to heroes and inspirational leaders.

Not a lot of people like the idea of putting their heads on the line but they love to hear stories of people who put their heads on the line.

So an effective instrument in your marketing toolbox is a star. By that, I mean someone respected in the community to feature in your ad, if you can afford it.

There is a reason why corporate giants like Nike or Coca cola spend billions each year on sponsoring stars to feature in their ads and wear their logos.

Star power is an effective marketing tool.

Big corporations have spent billions testing this hypothesis; they know it works, which is why they continue do it.

So you can take advantage of the information without spending billions of your own.

You Need Good Story

The second effective psychological marketing tool is story. As I intimated previously, we have all been conditioned from small to love stories.

Our parents' first forms of communication with us were in the form of stories.

Many of us went to bed with bedtime stories each night when we were kids.

As adults, many of the affiliations we make whether it is our choice of work or our sport teams are based on the stories we tell ourselves.

Every religious book is filled with stories.

It is those stories people buy that they are sometimes willing to harm their fellow human being.

In his book 'All Marketers Are Liar', author Seth Godin pointed to the fact that all of our buying decisions are based upon the stories we tell ourselves about the products and services we buy.

He gave the example of a very expensive wine glass that many wine drinkers believe makes the wine taste better. There is no evident that the makers of the wine glass added some special technology or chemical when making the glass to change the taste of the wine in it.

Yet perfectly rational people believe that drinking wine from that glass makes the wine taste better.

What really tastes better is the story behind the glass. The story the glassmakers tell wine drinkers about his glass.

Political elections are won on the strength of the personal stories of candidates. Their abilities to connect to voters' heart with their personal stories can be the difference between winning and losing an election campaign.

For us small business owners, without a strong brand identify, what we really have to sell is our personal stories. Our personal stories can make the difference between us making a sale and not making it.

You Need Good Solution

The final part of using psychology to market your products or services is your solutions.

It does not matter what you are selling, whether it is a product or service, what the prospect is buying from you is a solution.

In previous sections, I listed what people buy from you so I am not going to repeat this point here.

But what you need to understand is people buy solutions to a problem, they do not buy your product or service.

Mathematics

The final part of your marketing process has to do with the measurement of the result.

The late American business philosopher Jim Rohn once said, when you ask someone how are you doing in life and they respond 'I don't know' you tell them let's count. 'Let's count how much money you have in your bank account, how much money you make at the end of the week or the month that will be a clear indication of how well you are doing'.

In management, there is a saying that anything that gets measured is improved.

Ninety-five percent of marketing campaigns fail.

The reason those marketing campaigns fail has nothing to do with the people running them or strategies used. It has to do with measurement of results.

The Two Types of Marketing

There are two types of marketing: Branding and direct response marketing.

Branding is basically getting your business known in the marketplace and direct response marketing is accountability marketing.

The majority of marketing agencies and businesses prefer branding because it cannot be measured.

If you watch ads on television or listen to radio ads, you will discover that most of them are just talking about the product or service without a clear call to action.

In the section about using your website as an effective marketing tool, I mentioned the fact that many businesses have brochure sites.

The reason they have brochure sites is because, it is impossible to measure the performance of the website.

When you have a lead generation site, if you are not generating leads from the site, you quickly know that your site is not performing the function for which it was designed. The same level of measurement is applied to every aspect of your marketing.

How to Measure Your Marketing

The first step in measuring your marketing result is to engage in direct response marketing instead of branding.

As the name implies, the aim of direct response marketing is to solicit a response. Therefore, the effectiveness of the marketing is based on the response you receive.

Every direct response marketing text has a call to action. A call to action is simply some type of action you expect your prospects to take after reading your marketing message.

The difference between the amount of messages that were sent out and the response you receive is the outcome of your marketing campaign.

> *If you sent out 100 letters and you receive 20 responses, then your marketing campaign produced a 20% response.*

If out of the 20 responses five bought your product or service then you had a five percent result from that particular marketing campaign.

However, the other significant figure you need to know is how much did it cost you to acquire those five customers?

With that information, you will be able to tell if your marketing campaign was a success. To arrive at that figure, you simply need to divide the total amount of sales by the amount spent on the entire campaign.

> Let's say you spent £100 to send out the hundred letters that gave you those five customers, your cost per customer acquisition will be £20 for each customer.
>
> If your cost per customer acquisition is £20 each for customers that paid you £100 each, your profit on each customer is £80.

This figure does not take into account repeat sales and referrals that might be come from those five.

However, having an idea of the amount it cost to acquire a customer will give you a good indication of the amount of resources you need to conduct your marketing and achieve your business goals.

There are few metrics that are critical for tracking and measuring your marketing efforts, knowing those metrics is important for your success as a business owner.

Workshop

1. How do you currently reach your prospects?

_____

_____

_____

2. What criteria did you use to determine if your current channel of communication is the most cost effective one?

_____

_____

_____

3. How many marketing channels to do you currently use to communicate your marketing message?

_____

_____

_____

4. Do you use both online and offline media to communicate your marketing message?

_____

_____

_____

5. What strategies do you employ to ensure your marketing message is opened and read?

_____

_____

_____

6. Do you currently engage in direct response marketing or branding?

_____

_____

_____

7. What type of website do you have, ecommerce, brochure or lead generation website?

_____

_____

_____

8. Do you drive traffic to your website, if you how? Do you depend on free traffic?

9. How effectively do you use social media, do you simply do free posting hoping to attract customer to your site?

10. Do you have mechanism in place for measurement of your marketing activities?

Summary

While visiting London a few months ago, I felt an excruciating toothache. I wanted to bear the pain until I returned to Manchester because my dentist is in Manchester.

But if you have ever had toothache you know that the pain does not reduce with time, it increases as time go on.

On my daily exercise routine, I had noticed the sign of a dental practice not far from where I was lodging. Therefore, with the pain intensifying by the minute, I decided to visit that dental surgery.

When I arrived at the clinic, I cringed at the thought of being treated in that surgery.

The doors were dirty, with dust that seemed like they had not been cleaned for the past fifty years. The front of the building was a complete mess.

As I stood in front of the building contemplating my options, a thought ran through my mind: who in their right mind will want to go into such a place for dental treatment?

Except of cause if they had death wish.

Or they were experiencing excruciating pain as I was experiencing.

The only other option opened to me at the time was going to the Accident & Emergency (A&E).

After weighing both options, I decided 'Dr. Death' (the dirty dental surgery) was the lesser of the two evils.

When I entered the surgery, I was a bit relieved because the inside looked clean as a medical facility supposed to appear.

However, when I went in to see the dentist, I noticed the equipment did not appear freshly cleaned. When I go to see my dentist in Manchester, I watch them open freshly cleaned equipment before my eyes.

Furthermore, the dentist wanted to touch me without wearing gloves. I had to insist he wore gloves.

After observing that, I thought to myself: this place is a morgue, there is no way I am going to accept treatment here.

Since I had already paid the consultation fees, I thought I might as well allow him to complete the x-ray and tell me the cause of my pain.

If it was something I could live with till I return to Manchester, then I would wait. If not and I was forced to go to the A&E, I will at least have my x-ray to show them.

After the x-ray, he told me the cause of my pain and suggested a treatment plan. I politely declined and quickly found my way out of there.

By the time I had completed the process with him, my pain had lessened.

Consequently, I waited till I returned to Manchester to see my dentist.

For all I know the guy could have been the most brilliant dentist in London.

But that was beside the point.

The entire process leading to the point at which he suggested the treatment plan had already sharped my perception of him and his surgery.

The dirty entrance, he wanting to examine me without gloves had already sharped my perception of the practice.

In marketing, perception is reality.

Your prospect's perception of you and your business will determine their response to your marketing message.

When I do consultation for retailers, I tell them the story of my visit to Harrods.

Harrods is a high end retail department store that attracts the who-is-who from around the world.

The first time I visited Harrods, I was expecting to rub shoulders with some celebrities. However, instead of meeting a royalty, what caught my attention was a red toy bus.

I had bought the same bus for my son in ASAD. It was the same red bus in the same packaging, probably made by the same people in the same factory in China, being sold in Harrods almost three times the price it was sold for in ASDA.

A thought popped into my mind.

Why was it that the same bus, in the same packaging being sold in Harrods almost three times the price I bought it for in ASDA?

As I walked around Harrods, the answer came to me.

The royalties, celebrities and billionaires who shop in Harrods do not shop there for the crappy made in China bus, they shop there for the experience of buying the bus.

What they buy in Harrods is the:

- Beautiful store design
- Attractive visual merchandise display
- Exceptional customer service

The surgery was missing what author Seth Godin called "free prize".

This was a dental practice for crying out loud.

In there, they open people's mouths. Through your mouth, you stand a high risk of contracting lots of bacterial that could be fatal.

My thought process was, if they could not be bothered to clean the entrance, how was I sure they even clean the equipment after use.

As I said, when I visit my dentist in Manchester, I always observe them open freshly cleaned equipment right before I eyes. This gives me the confident that they care.

It did not matter how cheap the London dental practice would have been, I would not have accepted treatment from there because the experience of the environment and the experience of the dentist had already prejudiced my perception of the surgery.

Will I recommend the surgery to anyone?

Hell no!

As I sat at the reception waiting to be called, I asked the receptionist out of curiosity if they engaged in any form of marketing. She responded that they did but marketing agencies just collect their money and their marketing activities never produce results.

As a result of that, they stopped marketing their practice.

I wonder why?

Why did I tell you this story?

Here is the point of the story, which is the theme of this book and the foundation upon which modern marketing rests: in the new marketing environment, the marketing is in the product and service.

This point is so important I am going to repeat it: in the new economy, marketing is in the product or service.

Marketing is no longer about placing ad in the yellow pages, newspapers, TV, radio or on the internet, marketing is about 'free prize' inside the product or service.

What do I mean by 'free prize'?

'Free prize' is the experience your customers and prospects derive when they interact with your business.

Example of 'free prize' is Harrods':

- Beautiful store design
- Attractive visual merchandise display
- Exceptional customer service

The dental receptionist was moaning that they spent thousands on marketing that did not produce results.

Little did she know that their dirty entrance frustrated their marketing efforts.

Modern marketing is about being remarkable and exceptional. Except if you own the Nikes and the McDonalds, you do not have the resources to do carpet bombing or interruption marketing any longer.

The average person is exposed to over two thousand marketing messages every single day.

Consumers are overwhelmed with thousands of marketing messages coming at them from every direction.

What they currently do is build defensive mechanisms that shields them from the onslaught of marketers like you and I.

There is the ever strengthening spam filters, the do not call list, the no junk mail, no solicitation and the list goes on.

So how can you break through all of those ever increasing marketing repellents consumers are constantly erecting?

Most importantly, how can you do it in the most cost-effective way?

The answer to these and many other questions is what I have tried to provide in this workbook.

75% of businesses fail before their tenth anniversary. If the owners of those failed businesses were surveyed as to why their businesses fail, they will blame difficult trading conditions.

The reality is this, every single business that fails, fail because of the lack of customers.

And the reason businesses struggle to attract customers is the majority of businesses engage in branding exercises.

Except you have a billion pound to spend on marketing, to engage in branding is tantamount to deliberately flossing your many down the drain.

Branding is for big corporations because they have the resources to stick to it until it works.

For us small businesses the most effective form of marketing that will work for us without fail if done well is direct response marketing.

Over a hundred years ago, John Wanamaker, the merchant king wrote: "Half the money I spend on advertising is wasted; the trouble is I don't know which half".

A few year after Mr. Wanamaker said those famous words, Claude Hopkins wrote in his classic book 'Scientific Advertising': "The time has come when advertising has in some hands reached the status of a science. It is based on fixed principles and is reasonably exact. The causes and effects have been analyzed until they are well understood."

It seems 'Scientific Advertising' is the only marketing book Amazon's founder Jeff Bezos ever read.

When I discussed conversion, I mentioned that Amazon has hundreds of staff whose only function is to study the activities of each and every visitor to their website, and they continue to tweak their website to respond to customer activities on the site.

The reason Amazon does this is they understand that accountability marketing or direct response marketing is the only effective form of marketing.

How can a business successfully implement direct response marketing?

Effective direct response marketing is about the three Ms:

- The market: who you are selling to?
- The message: what you are selling?
- The media: how you are going to sell to them

You cannot effectively sell your product or service if you do not know who you are selling to.

Choosing the right target audience increases your chance of success by about 50%.

When you have selected your target audience, the next step in the process is, how do you communicate your marketing message to them?

How do you ensure that when they see your marketing message, your leaflet, your website or brochure, they know instantly that the message is for them?

After you have crafted an effective marketing message, how do you reach them with your message?

The strategies for reaching them with your marketing message is the third step in the marketing triangle.

Those three steps for effective marketing is what this book has been about. I have walked you through the process of crafting your marketing message, identifying your target audience and selecting the right media through which to channel your marketing message.

I have also focused on the three Ss:

- Star
- Story
- Solution

Marketing is about people. When someone remove their wallet to buy your product or service, what they are buying is not the physical product or the service you are providing them.

What they are buying is you, the story you told them and the story they tell themselves about it.

So as you created your marketing message, do not ignore the fact that they are buying you, your story and the solution your product or service represent to them.

Finally, anything that gets measured gets improved.

You will be unable to evaluate the results of your marketing without mechanisms for testing and measuring each and every step of the process.

In the workbook, I provided you the types of data to collect and the means of going about measuring them.

Marketing is the lifeblood of any business. Without marketing, a business will not survive.

Marketing has evolved. Strategies and tactics that were once effective are no long relevant in this new dispensation.

However, marketing fundamentals remains and will remain constant till the end of time.

What I have given you in this workbook are marketing fundamentals that if deployed correctly will change your business and your life.

"A lobster, when left high and dry among the rock, does not have the sense enough to work his way back to the sea, but waits for the sea to come to him. If it does not come, he remains where he is and dies, although the slightest effort would enable him to reach the waves, which are perhaps within a yard of him. The world is full of human lobsters; people stranded on the rocks of indecision and procrastination, who, instead of putting forth their own energies, are waiting for some grand billow of good fortune to set them afloat"

Don't let this be you.

I hope you take action on the information you have learnt in this workbook!

Great Books by Romeo

Book Romeo now!

+44 (0)20 8798 0579

romeo@theprofitexperts.co.uk

27.9% The Most Effective Retail Shrinkage Reduction Technologies

Prior to investing in any technology, there are vital questions that need to answered; those questions along with their answers can be found in this e-book.

This e-book was conceived out of our own desperate efforts to answer those questions.

What you will learn:

- Technologies That Prevent Employee Theft
- Technologies That Prevent Shoplifting
- Receiving Technologies
- Multi-purpose Technologies

12.24% The Most Effective Retail Employee Error Reduction Strategies

Employee errors in pricing, accounting and receiving contribute approximately 18% of retail shrinkage; this equates to £18,623 in losses to an average supermarket or store and almost £49,679 in losses to a superstore. This means that a store or supermarket that operates with a 1% net profit will need to make an additional £3million in annual sales in order to recover profit lost due to employee errors. By the same measure a typical hyper store will need to increase its sales by £8million.

You will learn:

- Constitutes as Retail Employee Error
- to Calculate the Cost of Employee Error
- to Calculate Additional Sales Required to Recover Losses Caused by Employee Error
- of Employee Error
- to Reduce Employee Error
- Ultimate Employee Error Prevention Formula
- to Apply the Lessons from This E-Book to Your Business

43.5% The Most Effective Retail Profit Protection Strategies

The retail landscape is changing rapidly with the constant increase in internet shopping. From 2005 to 2009, the online shopping population grew to 1.6 billion.

It is predicted to rise to 2.3 billion by 2014 with gross revenue totalling $778.6 billion. This is bad news for traditional brick and mortar retail businesses.

The question is: are you prepared? You will find your answer in this eBook.

What you will learn:

- The Conventional Approach to Loss prevention
- Why Loss Prevention is Critical to Retail
- Loss Prevention Spending vs Return on Investment
- What You Are Losing
- Profit vs Sales Calculation
- How to Create a Culture of Loss Prevention
- Effective Shrinkage Management Strategies
- The Ultimate Profit Protection Formula

24.5% The Most Effective Perishable And Non-Perishable Shrinkage Reduction Strategies

This e-book is jam packed with information on the causes of retail shrinkage, types of retail shrinkage, the cost of shrinkage to the retail industry and how shrinkage can be prevented. It is a comprehensive e-book on how and why shrinkage occurs and it provides a step-by-step guide on how to prevent shrinkage.

You will learn:

- An Introduction to Perishable Shrinkage
- Breakdown of Perishable Shrinkage
- Causes of Perishable Shrinkage
- How to Prevent Perishable Shrinkage
- The Ultimate Perishable Shrinkage Prevention Formula
- An Introduction to Non-Perishable Shrinkage
- Classification of Non-Perishable Shrinkage
- Breakdown of Non-Perishable Shrinkage
- Strategies for Preventing Non-Perishable Shrinkage
- The Ultimate Non-Perishable Shrinkage Prevention Formula
- How to Apply The Lessons From This E-Book to Your Business

27.8% The Most Effective Retail Employee Theft Reduction Strategies

The majority of retail employees are decent people who go to work each day to serve their customers and make their living.

However, there are the rotten apples that contaminate the good names of the rest.

This e-book is an instructional guide to retailers to show them how to minimise and prevent employee theft in their stores. Like shoplifting most incidents of employee theft occur because the opportunity exists. When retailers remove the opportunity, they can reduce the possibilities. This e-book will show retailers how to remove the opportunities that allow employee theft in their stores.

You will learn:

- Why Employees Steal
- The Process of Employee Theft
- Signs of Employee Theft
- How to Calculate the Cost of Employee Theft
- How to Prevent Employee Theft
- How Technology Can Help Prevent Employee Theft
- The Ultimate Employee Theft Prevention Formula

84%: The Most Effective Strategies for Increasing Retail Profit

The formula for increasing profit in retail is to increase sales and reduce shrinkage. How can retailers increase sales and reduce shrinkage? The answer is in this book.

You will learn everything you need to know about:

- Creating a Culture of Loss Prevention
- Employee Error
- Employee Theft
- Shoplifting
- Perishable and Non-Perishable Shrinkage
- Receiving Shrinkage
- Technologies that Help to Reduce Retail Shrinkage

Visual Merchandise: How to Create a Beautiful Yet Profitable Display

Merchandise display is the most effective form of advertising for a retail store. The more attractive a display, the higher the possibility of increasing sales. This book will show retailers how to create a display that is so attractive that it would increase their footfall tenfold.

You will learn:

- The psychology behind visual merchandising
- How to use visual merchandising to increase retail sales
- Challenges facing visual merchandisers
- How to burst the price myth with creative merchandise display
- The best merchandise display strategies
- How to maximise display space allocation with creative fixtures
- The pros and cons of using a planogram
- The pros and cons of hiring visual merchandising companies
- Most effective visual merchandise technologies
- How to display merchandise for maximum profit

Store Design Blueprint: How to Design an Attractive But Profitable Store

There are three fundamental principles that underpin a retail store design:

1. Attract customers as they pass by the store
2. Entice them to enter the store
3. Persuade them to buy

The aim of this book is to show retailers how to apply these principles to this store design.

You will learn:

- Store design psychology – what you must know to succeed
- Store design – Image selling
- How to use store design to increase sales
- Store design for increased customer flow
- Choosing your store colour and layout
- The best retail store lighting system
- How to wow customers with creative storefront design
- How to choose the right materials for store design
- Designing store for profit – design security
- Store design technologies

How to Market and Manage A Professional Firm Series: How to make 7 Figure annually as a doctor, dentist, accountant, lawyer, consultant and private security firm owner.

There are four elements essential for the success of any business:

1. Visionary leadership
2. Great people
3. Good system
4. Good marketing system

In the How to Market and Manage A Professional Firm Series, we teach professional entrepreneurs how to effectively utilize these four elements for the development of their businesses.

Many professionals are good technicians. They are good at their professions, however, when it comes to running business they are challenged.

The aim of the 7 Figure Code Books Series is to show professionals how to enhance their technical skills and apply similar levels of structural thinking into building a 7 Figure business.

There is no reason why a doctor or lawyer should not be able to easily make 7 Figure per annum. We show them how to achieve this in the How to Market and Manage A Professional Firm Series.

You will learn:

- How to create an effective business system that runs on auto-pilot
- How to recruit and retain only top talents
- How to develop an effective marketing system
- How to create new market for a product or service
- How the attract new clients and retain existing ones

Book Romeo

Book Romeo now by calling:
+44(0)78 650 49508
Or email: romeo@theprofitexperts.co.uk

www.ingramcontent.com/pod-product-compliance
Lightning Source LLC
Chambersburg PA
CBHW051644170526
45167CB00001B/327